The Four Week Financial Turnaround

A Monthly Budgeting Workbook for the Household
Create a simple plan that works for you.

DEREK C. OLSEN

THOUGHTS FROM A FEW FRIENDS OF MINE:

"As a life coach I see many people who have created strategies for career success. But those same people frequently have no plan for handling the money generated by that career success. In *The Four Week Financial Turnaround*, Derek Olsen shares clear systems and processes for being as intentional about success in your finances as you would expect in business. With no plan in place, your finances – and your business – will likely fail. Don't take that chance."

— Dan Miller
Creative thinker at 48days.net
Author of *48 Days to the Work You Love*
48days.com

"Derek Olsen takes a practical, funny, real-life approach to fixing your budgeting woes once and for all. He doesn't pretend it's easy, but you'll think it's much easier after reading *The Four Week Financial Turnaround* and putting its lessons into practice."

— Joshua Fields Millburn
TheMinimalists.com

"Derek knows what he's talking about when it comes to both finances and life! I am so impressed with what he's put together. Bottom line, it's the total package. Way to go, Derek!"

— Kent Julian
LiveItForward.com

"Derek's tools are straightforward and easy to use. His compelling writing style and fast-action financial exercises motivate you to sit down and work through the important stuff in order to get on track with where you want to go financially. I recommend Derek's tools to anyone looking to get a better grip on their financial situation and create a future of personal and familial prosperity."

— Ted Gonder
Co-founder and Executive Director, Moneythink
MoneyThink.org

"Give yourself the gift of *The Four Week Financial Turnaround*. In a straightforward fashion, Derek Olsen guides you through a personal finance transformation. With conscious effort, some dedication, and practicing Derek's personal budgeting system, you can change your future. Live life abundantly; start with *The Four Week Financial Turnaround*."

— **Connie Williams**
Author of *THiNking Consciously Rocks!*
Co-Host of Connie and Sheila Talk: Real Life, Real Estate, Real Fun
ConnieAndSheilaTalk.com

"When you consider starting a new exercise routine, do you look to your slightly overweight family member whose idea of working out is their multiple trips to the pantry? Or do you seek the advice of someone that has hands-on experience and knowledge in the field of fitness? It's a no-brainer! Building financial strength and stability should be no different. Derek and Carrie Olsen have lived, breathed and endured financial turmoil through a short sale. They have first-hand knowledge of what it takes to overcome financial demise and have taken the necessary steps to begin building their strong financial future."

— **Cindy Cook**
TheCindyCookTeam.com

"Purchasing a financial workbook isn't something I'd ever really considered doing - until I came across this powerful resource from Derek and Carrie. As a result of getting my hands on this fantastic budgeting workbook, my wife and I have been able to work out a budget that fits us really well. I love Derek's casual, no-nonsense, practical approach to this whole issue. I feel so much more confident in our financial direction than before. I'm actually excited about where we're headed as a family. I'm not afraid to talk about money. I highly, HIGHLY recommend this! Getting to know Derek and Carrie has been one of the highlights of my year. I'm so glad I took the time!"

— **Joshua Gordon**
JoshuaGordon.net
TheNonConformistFamily.com

The Four Week Financial Turnaround
First Edition

Beatnik Publishing, a division of Olsen & Olsen Financial, LLC.
Kansas City, MO

www.BeatnikBudget.com

ISBN-10: 0985886307
ISBN-13: 978-0985886301

Contact information can be found at www.DerekCOlsen.com
More information about this workbook can be found at www.FourWeekFinancialTurnaround.com

This book is intended for use as a general guide to help you, the reader, take control of your money and your spending habits. This book is not a substitute for legal advice, tax planning, retirement planning, or other financial planning or accounting services. Please consult your attorney, accountant, or other licensed professional for specific questions regarding your personal situation. This book is strictly for entertainment and informational purposes only and is not to be considered a substitute for professional financial planning. Any results, good or bad, that occur as a result of taking action on the suggestions, stories, information, recommendations, and advice given in this book are not the responsibility of the author.

10 9 8 7 6 5 4 3 2 1

PEOPLE WHO HELPED BRING THIS WORK TO LIFE
(Acknowledgements)

Without the following people, plus many others, this work
would still be just a bunch of thoughts in my mind.
Thank You!

- ❖ Priceless love and support: Carrie Olsen – HisPlusHersEqualsOurs.com
- ❖ Photo: Rachel Porter – LoveIsRising.blogspot.com
- ❖ Editing: Angie Pederson – AngiePedersen.typepad.com
- ❖ Editing: Lauren Forest – WordPerfectionist.com
- ❖ Cover: Ben Brunner – By Request
- ❖ Formatting & layout design: Carrie Olsen
- ❖ Graphics: Stefanie Zehnder – StefanieZehnder.com
- ❖ Media kit: Stefanie Zehnder

Many, many thanks to The Book Launch Team. It was fun, wasn't it?
Just like I promised.

Family, friends and the rest, you know who you are. Thanks.

To My
Book Launch Team,
Its Going to be Fun,
Promise!
—Derek

CONTENTS

INTRODUCTION

Here I am having fun with the wife, Carrie.
(Pro marriage tip: marry your best friend!)

Life doesn't come with an owner's manual. I've had to rely on trial and error – which means a lot of trials and a lot of errors. In other words, a lot of experiences I'd prefer not to repeat. I wouldn't trade them in, but I am glad they are in the past.

Experience is the best teacher, which means I've been taught a lot! And I have lots of lessons to share. Read more about my journey at BeatnikBudget.com/story.

I've taken my background in business management and combined it with the zest of entrepreneurship. I've added them together with my love of helping people solve their money problems so they can achieve their financial goals.

The result is this book. A book designed to help make your life easier.

I'd like to offer you the system I developed over the past several years. It has (almost) everything I've learned about how to create and manage a financial plan for the average, everyday normal person. Nothing complicated – just a simple plan that works.

-Derek

GETTING STARTED:
SETTING YOUR COURSE FOR SUCCESS

Where We're Headed

It's always a good idea to begin with the end in mind – to know where we're going before we take the first step. That way we can move in the right direction, stay focused, gain momentum along the way, and know when we've arrived. No walking in circles.

Think of our work here as a journey. The destination is freedom, empowerment, and control over your finances. If you stick with my system, you'll get to this destination. But you'll also get something more. You'll get the real prize, which is peace of mind.

Imagine waking up in the morning feeling completely at ease, knowing the chaos and uncertainty surrounding your money is gone for good. Imagine sleeping the whole night through, rather than being jolted awake by the question of whether you paid a bill on time (or if there was enough in your account to cover it).

Make the Time

Get your calendar out and schedule one hour per week for the next four weeks. Label that time, "Investing in the success of my financial future." Realize that you have the time to do this. The results that come from completing this workbook are infinitely more valuable than the time you will spend working through it.

Stick with this system and you'll get the real prize, which is peace of mind.

You will quickly realize that the time spent is not a cost but rather an investment, an investment that will pay dividends for the rest of your life. Sign up for the *Four Week Financial Turnaround* email course. You will get one email each week for the next four weeks. Those emails will remind you where you are in the process and keep you moving forward. Think of it as your very own accountability partner. Sign up by visiting BeatnikBudget.com/workshops. This four-week e-course is fun and will help keep you motivated to finish this workbook. It's free and it's fun, start today.

Hi, I'm Derek…and I'll Be Your Tour Guide

This workbook is your road map, and I'll be your tour guide for the journey. Here's what we'll accomplish together:

- *Create a starting point.* Many people have told me they don't have a financial strategy because they don't know where to start. It's understandable because without a clear starting point the process can feel overwhelming. You can breathe easy because this workbook will help you create your starting point. Getting started is half the battle. Have you been avoiding getting started? Avoid no more.

- *Follow the path.* The numbered worksheets and step-by-step instructions in this workbook provide clear direction. The Four Week Financial Turnaround Checklist is a great tool to keep you on the path. You'll find it at the end of this chapter. Just like following good directions, the checklist will take you all the way to your destination. What was that destination again? Oh yeah, *peace of mind.*

- *Discover information, knowledge, and tools.* When I say "information and knowledge" I'm talking about the hands-on side of this process that takes you all the way to the finish line. Throughout our journey we'll stay focused on *action-oriented information and knowledge*, not just theory and good ideas. Think of each worksheet as a different tool that has a different function. Each tool has its own purpose along the way. Knowing how to use the tool is half the equation, using the tool well is the other half.

To complete a project, you need the instructions and the right tools. You must know how to use the tools, and most importantly, *you must take action.* You also need a good reason why and some motivation. There are plenty of great reasons why and lots of motivation throughout this book.

This workbook will keep you in action mode. And as your tour guide, I'll be here to support you along the way.

Are We There Yet?

Earlier we talked about knowing where we're headed. We talked about how freedom, empowerment, and control are the destination. We also talked about the real prize, peace of mind.

You may be wondering what that will look like when you've achieved it. In other words, how will you know you have arrived at your destination?

Recognizing Your Success

There is a huge payoff that will result from spending a few weeks working through this material. Your life will dramatically improve in these ways:

You will…

- Manage your monthly budget so well it becomes "second nature."
- Feel confident and optimistic about your overall financial situation.
- Easily revise your overall financial picture by applying the lessons you've learned.
- Have greater control over the way you spend your hard-earned money.
- Escape the trap of living paycheck to paycheck.
- Pay off debt and be rid of that burden, once and for all.
- Build a cash savings for added stability.
- Be able to invest in a secure financial future.
- Have more confidence in your financial decisions and financial future.
- Have an organized plan of action that you feel great about.
- Have more harmony in your relationships and family life.
- Be a happier and healthier you.
- Believe it or not, have fun along the way!

Sounds great, right? Yeah, it's pretty great.

Celebrate your milestones

You will recognize your continuing success, and it is important to celebrate it, too. After each step along the way, we will celebrate your progress together. Realize that you are making progress, and reward yourself during this journey.

Is This Book Right for You?

I would hate to lead you down a path that you aren't up for traveling down or give you tools that you don't need. So, let's make sure you have the right workbook.

Although we do spend time crunching the numbers, it's not the focal point of this workbook. We go beyond number crunching as a way to create change and measure the results of that change. If you are looking for a book full of math and equations, you are cold, very cold. We will use math as a tool, but we go deeper in this book.

If you are looking for detailed information on investing, retirement, insurance, mortgages, and estate planning, you have the wrong book. I believe in all of these things. My family and I have these tools working for us. However, they simply aren't covered in this workbook. This workbook sets you up to be able to use those tools later.

If you want to be more organized, and if you need to spend some time creating order out of chaos, this workbook is definitely for you.

While these things are important – very important – you can't put $200 a month into a mutual fund if you already spent it. Control your money first and teach it to "do tricks" second. This book will focus on the decisions that you make with your money while it is in your hands.

If you want to be more organized, and if you need to spend some time creating order out of chaos, *The Four Week Financial Turnaround* is definitely for you. The insight you gain from completing this workbook will compel you to reconsider the way you are spending your hard-earned money. This workbook will help you evaluate the reasons why you spend your money the way you do. You will then be able to implement new ways to spend, save, give, and invest your hard-earned money.

Rearranging numbers on a spreadsheet is helpful and we will also do some of that. We will then come up with lots of reasons to rearrange those numbers. Doing this, along with pre-monthly budget thinking and planning, is a powerful way to teach yourself how to consider the possible results of your spending choices. The key to successful decision-making is the ability to know the likely outcome before taking action.

Success Is a Habit: What's This Book Really About?

There are only two ways to have more money: earn more or spend less.

This workbook is about creating healthy spending habits. Notice I said spending rather than earning. Most people think that having more money will solve their money problems. Unfortunately, they have very little (if any) control over how much money they earn. (At least in the short term.) The only other choice is to plan well and control the money that they do earn. Making smart choices when deciding how to spend and save is the solution to solving those money problems.

I imagine you are making more money now than you did 5, 10, or 20 years ago. Did that solve your money issues or did those issues follow you and grow along with your paycheck? Earning more money is usually a good idea, but not always the answer.

If you don't have a plan for managing the money you earn now, chances are that you won't have a plan for the money you earn in the future. This means it's time to create one. Why not start now? If you can't lift a 20 pound weight, a 50 pound weight isn't the answer. Put another way, a larger audience isn't the answer to your bad dance moves.

Learn these money management skills now and you will be better able to manage your millions in the future. The skills, knowledge, tools, and behavior will not change, only the numbers you plug into the calculator and budget spreadsheet will change. These skills are highly transferrable to any financial situation, no matter the size of the paycheck. If you learn how to properly manage $30,000, you will know how to properly manage $300,000. The skills are the same for any amount of money.

This workbook has a heavy emphasis on questioning your spending and saving behavior. Let this workbook encourage you to question your current financial patterns. You'll make decisions based on what is truly important and what is less so. This is a journey of deconstructing the habits that aren't working and reconstructing new habits that will work better. Together we will question the status quo. If you would like to improve your financial situation, this workbook will help you come up with creative ways to produce new results. Go behind the scenes and explore the reasons why you spend your money the way you do. If those reasons aren't helping you accomplish your financial goals, perhaps it is time to create some new reasons. Perhaps you spend your money the way you do because you don't have much of a plan. Perhaps you need to be pro-active instead of just feeling your way through the weeks, months, and years.

You must start by believing that this will work.
So, believe.

You can start spending less money today – this very minute. If you don't have control over the amount of money you make, controlling the way you spend is the only way to improve your finances. When you start aligning your spending habits with your vision of financial success, you will see immediate results. Don't wait for your paycheck to double. That could take years. Take charge of what you have now. Start today.

But Derek, I've Already Tried Spending Less!

I hear that objection a lot. You may already be doing your best to manage your money well. If you're like most people it's not working as well as you would like, despite your best efforts. Perhaps you don't know what else to cut out of your budget. Everything you spend your money on seems like a necessary expense.

So here's the good news. You're not alone with that problem. Here's the better news. This book will solve that problem. We will approach this puzzle in powerful ways that truly work. Each worksheet is a piece of the puzzle. And once you've put all the pieces together you'll start feeling great about the new financial picture you see. You must start this process by believing that there is room for improvement. All you have to do is find it and make it work. You must start by believing that this will work. So, believe.

At first we'll need to dig in deep to discover the areas where improvement is possible. That is the only way to make real progress and lasting change. Think of these four weeks as an investment in your future. The ongoing results will create the lasting security you want for you and your family.

Get to the root cause

It's not enough to ask, "What can I cut from my budget?" Ask yourself two more questions and the answers will uncover new ways to think about how you spend and save your money.

You have heard the expression, "The root of the problem." What does that mean and how can it help us during this process?

Anyone who has done a little gardening or lawn maintenance knows exactly what it means to get to the root of the problem. If you pull an unwanted weed from your garden and don't pull the entire root out of the ground the weed will grow back. It isn't enough to cut the weed all the way down to the ground. You must get the entire root system – including the parts below the ground. In other words, you must dig deeper and get to the reason why that root has the ability to re-grow. Your problem weed will grow back if the root of the problem isn't located and dealt with. Our work together here will teach you how to deny the weeds the ability to grow in the first place. Fewer roots means fewer weeds. By taking care of the roots, you won't have to even think about that weed again. Less time spent cutting down weeds allows for more time growing other plants and flowers.

Each step we take together I will ask you two important questions. These two questions will help you get to the root cause of each concept that we will explore. I don't want you to waste your time cutting down the same weed again and again. Let's get to the root cause and take care of those unwanted weeds once and for all. Then we can spend our time growing a healthier garden.

I will ask these two questions after most worksheets, modifying them for the situation.

Question 1: Why?

Why do you spend your money the way you do?

Everyone spends their money in different ways. There are as many different reasons why as there are people in the world, and everyone is different and unique. Perhaps your reasons need another look. Perhaps your reasons for spending your money the way you do are hard to define. Well thought out reasons bring clarity and purpose to your financial decisions. Good reasons lead to good choices that produce good results.

For example, let's say you don't exercise enough and you often stay up late watching TV. When you wake up in the morning you're typically tired and running late for work. Because you are tired you feel like you need two cups of coffee to start the day. And because you are usually running late you don't have enough time to make coffee at home. Consequently, you go to the drive-through coffee shop every morning on your way to work. This adds up to $100 a month. You have been doing this for years and it has become a habit. You do it without thinking.

It's easy to recognize that you need to spend less on coffee, especially if the $100 per month expense is preventing you from making progress in other areas. The results of cutting out the daily coffee are obvious. However, it can be difficult to make the appropriate changes without considering the reasons why you are over-spending on coffee. Attempting to make changes without understanding why is difficult and will leave you frustrated, even if you do manage to make the changes. If you only give up the coffee and don't address the reasons why you need the coffee, you put yourself in a worse situation.

So you give up the coffee. Now you are tired, running late and have no coffee to help get you through the day. The extra $100 a month is nice, but you don't feel like it is worth it because the cause of the situation has not been properly dealt with.

Let's go deeper than simply spending less on coffee, and ask "Why?" Why do I feel like I need the coffee? Answer: You're not exercising enough and you're staying up too late. Those are the reasons why you spend $100 a month on coffee. And that is why you aren't investing as much as you could into your mutual fund.

At first those reasons why (staying up late and no exercise), seem far removed from the results (spending $100 a month on coffee and not investing in your mutual fund). More often than not we only try to repair the damage instead of addressing the root cause. Constantly repairing unnecessary damage is always frustrating.

The frustration comes as a result of being trapped in a system that isn't working. If you address the root cause of the problem and deal with it properly, there will be no damage to repair, no weeds that re-grow. When there is no damage to repair, you eliminate the source of frustration. In other words, create a system that works and the frustration will disappear.

Only dropping the coffee is like cutting the weed down to the ground without pulling up the root. Getting some exercise and getting to sleep earlier will eliminate the need for the drive-through coffee. Like pulling up the root, there are no more weeds to deal with.

When you find and address the reasons why (the root cause), you can easily make real progress that will create lasting change.

Question 2: What are the consequences?

Another related question to ask yourself is this: *"What else could I do with this dollar?"*

Imagine asking (and answering) that question every time you spend a dollar. Literally think of all the other things you could do with that dollar. This will get your thinking on the right path quickly! Each dollar can only be spent once. For every dollar you spend in one category, you have one less dollar to spend elsewhere. Financial management is really just a series of choices, each choice leads to or away from a myriad of different outcomes.

> *When we pay attention to likely outcomes, we reclaim our power to direct our lives.*

Do you ever find yourself saying, *"I don't have enough money for that?"* That is only half of the truth. (The end result or consequence of some previous root cause.) The other half is that you likely DID have the money at one point in time. You chose to spend that money on something else. Granted, you may have spent that money on something reasonable and necessary like your mortgage payment or food. But how many poorly planned purchases did you make this month? How many of those purchases were made without much thought as to the consequences? How much of that could have been allocated towards larger, more meaningful purchases instead?

Right or wrong, good or bad, each choice we make has an outcome. The results of your financial choices don't just happen, they happen for a reason. Those results add up to create your current financial situation at any given moment in time.

> *When you address the reasons why, you can easily make real progress that will create lasting change.*

Every decision has positive or negative consequences. In most cases we can come to an accurate conclusion about what the outcome will be and how those consequences will affect us. Once we have identified the likely outcome, we have the power to adjust our choices accordingly. All of which we can do prior to taking action. In other words, when we pay attention to likely outcomes, we reclaim our power to direct our lives. We choose our futures based on the decisions we make each day. We choose the outcomes by deciding what choices to make. I don't know about you, but to me that is exciting. That makes me feel powerful and in charge. This workbook will help you choose how to use all of that decision making power.

Keep the Two Questions in Mind

These two questions are foundational to this budgeting method. They are ingrained in the very fiber of this workbook and are repeated throughout.

These two questions deal with the past. However, I don't recommend dwelling on the past. Spend just enough time there in order to gather the information you need to learn from. Then make the choice to leave the past *in the past*.

Use the answers to these two questions to help you figure out what to change, and then let this workbook help you make those changes. Decide to create a new future and move forward quickly. Do not drag the things that aren't working into the future with you. Drop them and leave them in the past. Replace those old habits with new ones that work better.

Choose to create a future that is full of the results you want, based on carefully constructed reasons why and positive intended consequences.

In order to have forward thinking, success driven thoughts and actions, ask these two questions:

1. *Why do I spend my money the way I do?* Do I have a good plan for spending my money? Does my plan help create a success-filled future that I am excited about? (Bringing you closer to your goals.)
2. *What else could I do with this dollar?* Will I experience healthy consequences as a result of this money management decision, and will it help create a success-filled future that I am excited about? (Again, bringing you closer to your goals.)

And speaking of a great future that you can get excited about, check out this next section…

A Raise? So Soon?

I love telling clients that before they know it, they'll be giving themselves a raise. Actually, I love it when they tell *me* that.

After just a few months using this money management method, most people say that they feel like they have gotten a raise. It's easy to imagine why they might feel that way. Imagine you have been living paycheck to paycheck for years. Then all of a sudden you have a few hundred — or several thousand — more dollars in the bank. How could you *not* feel like you got a raise?

After just one year, you can see how major progress is possible. How much debt could you pay off with these results? Could you save up to pay cash for your next car? How would you feel knowing that you have more financial breathing room?

Again, your situation is unique and the results might not be the same for you. I guarantee that you will see and be happy with the improvements you make as a result of using this budgeting method.

And remember, it's not just more money in the bank that we are after. We want to feel good, have confidence, and enjoy our money too.

YOUR FINANCIAL TURNAROUND TOOLBOX

The Worksheets

The weekly worksheets will help you organize your thoughts, goals, and actions. Each worksheet section includes an introduction with instructions, the worksheet itself, and a debriefing summary. All good travelers celebrate their milestones along the way (and take breaks to re-charge and re-focus), and we will too. Each debriefing section also helps you take a minute to see how to implement the lesson and how it will benefit you. We will talk about setting expectations and goals for the week, followed by a summary and conclusion.

Free PDF

Your toolbox includes a free download! No need for an eraser every time you want to make changes. Download the interactive PDF version of this workbook. Make changes, corrections, and mistakes all day long. Use it over and over. Download it at BeatnikBudget.com/FreeFourWeekPDF.

The Audio

This workbook comes with a BONUS four part audio series. This audio series is a great way to bring the weekly concepts to life. Listen to each week's audio after you have completed the week's worksheets. Download each .mp3 file at BeatnikBudget.com/FourWeekAudio.

Extra BONUS Time!

Shhh… There is a super-secret page on BeatnikBudget.com. A page with lots of helpful resources, products, and downloads. All of the stuff there is free and constantly being updated. Check the page often for updates.
BeatnikBudget.com/Bonus.
Shhh… Let's keep it between us.

Email Course

Jump all the way in and sign up for the *Four Week Financial Turnaround* email course. This e-course will keep you on track with a series of emails, one a week for four weeks. It's a great way to stay motivated and have fun during this journey. Sign up at BeatnikBudget.com/Workshops.

Remember, Your Tour Guide Is Here to Help

This workbook is your map and I am your tour guide for the journey.

That means questions, comments, suggestions, thoughts, and success stories are welcome and encouraged. I love hearing about my readers' progress.

Email	Derek@beatnikbudget.com
Website	BeatnikBudget.com
Website	FourWeekFinancialTurnaround.com
Twitter	@DerekCOlsen
Pinterest	pinterest.com/DerekCOlsen
Google +	Mr.DerekOlsen
Linked In	LinkedIn.com/in/DerekCOlsen
Facebook	Facebook.com/mr.derekolsen
Amazon	Amazon.com/author/DerekCOlsen

For the Beatnik media experience:

Watch	BeatnikBudget.com/video
Listen	BeatnikBudget.com/fourweekaudio

Enough talk already—let's get busy.

THE FOUR WEEK FINANCIAL TURNAROUND CHECKLIST

Fill out the worksheets in the order listed below and you will arrive in no time. Check off each worksheet as you complete it.

Worksheet Name	Page	Completed
Week One:		
#1 *Basic Assessment*	4	☐
#2 *Debt*	8	☐
#3 *Assets*	12	☐
#4 *Assets – Debts = Net Worth*	16	☐
Week Two:		
#5 *What Is My Cash Savings For?*	27	☐
#6 *The Cash Only System*	33	☐
#7 *Unplug*	38	☐
#8 *STOP It!*	42	☐
#9a *Is This Appropriate?*	49	☐
#9b *Appropriate Changes*	50	☐
#10 *Preliminary Budget*	55	☐
Week Three:		
#11 *Sell It for Cash*	66	☐
#12 *Extra Income*	70	☐
#13 *Attack Debt*	75	☐
#14 *Survive, Maintain, Thrive*	80	☐
#15 *Make It Automatic*	84	☐
Week Four:		
#16 *The Monthly Budget*	92	☐

The Four Week Financial Turnaround

Week One

WEEK ONE: AN ASSESSMENT

Starting point: Where are you now?

Introduction and goal: This week you will shed some light on your current financial location. If you are lost in a city and need to get somewhere, the first step is to find out where you are now. You would pull out a map and find your current location. In the same way, you will figure out where you are now, financially speaking.

Think of this week as answering two questions:

1. Where am I?
2. How did I get here?

Retrace your steps in order to get to a place that is a more suitable starting point. Sometimes it is necessary to take a quick look back in order to move forward.

Step 1: Basic Assessment

> ## Worksheet Goal: Begin organizing and tracking how you spend your hard-earned money.

For many people, this worksheet will be a challenge; for some it will be a breeze. If you already know all the figures needed for this first worksheet, great! You can move along fairly quickly. If this form is challenging for you, however, that's okay. You are far from alone. If your eyes aren't already open to the reality of your financial situation, Worksheet #1 will do the trick.

You'll need to hunt down a few pieces of information for this worksheet.

- Your paycheck and all other sources of income.
- Information about all of your bills, debts, and payments.
- A bank statement that shows every transaction from last month.

Directions: Record your income and then track where each dollar went.

1. Print off or view online your bank statement for last month.

2. Start with a sheet of scratch paper. You can also use your word processor, Excel, or a typewriter if that's your style. Go through each transaction on your bank statement and write down the spending category it belongs to. List the spending categories horizontally across the top of the scratch paper. For reference, use the categories listed on Worksheet #1 and then add your own categories as needed. (Categories will be expanded in the monthly budget.) See image on page 3 for an example scratch sheet of paper.

3. Now that you have the categories listed on the scratch paper, go through your bank statement and list each expense under the correct category heading. As you go through your account statement, remember to put a check mark next to each transaction as you write it down. Make sure you include everything.

4. Total up the amounts for each category and then write the category total on the worksheet. For example, if you have 14 transactions for food purchases at the grocery store, add them all up to get the total for the groceries category. Then record the total grocery amount on Worksheet #1.

There is no need to spend hours tracking down every penny. Just get as close as you can. It does not have to be perfect the first time. If it turns out messy and the numbers don't add up perfectly, relax. It will get better each month. If you don't have exact numbers for some items, just make an estimate of the average monthly expense. Also, round to the nearest dollar.

We are only working with the cash that actually hits your bank account. Everything that happens before hitting the bank account will be left outside the monthly budget. (This includes things like taxes and 401(k) contributions.) It is wise and recommended to pay close attention to these things but they will not be included within the monthly budget.

At the bottom of the worksheet, your total spending should equal your income to the dollar. If you are unsure what to do with a bit of spending that doesn't quite fit into a category, throw it in the "All Other/Mystery" line. You might end up with a big "Other/Mystery" amount. That's okay for now; as you continue to do your monthly budget, the numbers will clear up and make more sense. We will deal with the mystery numbers later. We will also add more detailed categories to this worksheet later.

Worksheet #1: Basic Assessment

Monthly income	$
Rent or mortgage	$
All monthly bills (e.g. utilities)	$
Car payment(s)	$
Loan payments (e.g. student loan)	$
Credit cards	$
All other debts	$
Groceries	$
Eating out	$
Clothing	$
Car – gasoline	$
Car – maintenance	$
Entertainment	$
Alcohol/cigarettes/vices	$
Pets/hobbies	$
Vacation/travel	$
Medical	$
Savings	$
Giving	$
Investing	$
Insurance	$
All other/mystery	$
Total spending	**$**
Subtract from income	**(Should = $0)**

Worksheet #1 Debrief

How did it go? Was it tough, easy? What did you learn?

Lots of people have no idea where their money goes each month. Most people are very surprised by what they learn. If you already do this every month and aren't surprised by what you find, you are a rare and precious gem – congrats. Even if that is you, there is always room for improvement. It is always a good idea to keep a close eye on your spending. Keep it up. If you did not learn anything new here, stay with me, this is only the beginning. We can't skip over the basics.

Your total spending should equal your income to the dollar. If you spent less than you made, the remainder should go into savings. If you spent more than you earned, that extra money came from one of two places:

1. *Your own cash reserve:* It is possible to spend more than you earned in a given month. Occasionally spending more than you earned in the same month is only advisable when you have enough savings to handle the expense. (More on this topic later.)

2. *Borrowed from an outside source such as a credit card or loan:* If you borrowed money this month to make ends meet, the amount that you borrowed should be thought of as borrowed income (or debt), not earned income. Please make a distinction between these two very different sources of income. (We will create a plan to attack any debt you might have later.)

Why is it so important that your budget equals zero? Your budget should equal zero so that you know for sure that you aren't out-spending your income and that you are fully allocating every dollar.

This worksheet is first for a reason. We need to discover where your money *has been* going before we can tell your money where *to go*.

Get to the root cause

- -

Take a minute to write down the "whys and consequences." Use the questions below to help you grab that weed and pull up its roots!

Name one specific area that you can improve on this month and how you plan to make those improvements.

_____

_____

_____

Name one specific area that you are doing well in. How can you continue to make progress here?

_____

_____

How can you improve your spending, saving and giving habits?

_____

_____

What is a specific result of improving your spending, saving and giving habits?

_____

_____

Celebrate your milestones

When you get a handle on your monthly expenses, that is an achievement on its own. This first step should be celebrated!

How does it feel to know you are on your way to having greater financial control and peace of mind?

_____

_____

What will being more organized allow you to accomplish?

_____

_____

Great job! Let's take a closer look at any debt you might have.

Step 2: List Your Debt

> Worksheet Goal: Take the first step towards becoming debt free. Find your debt-free target number.

Grab your computer and dig up all those lost and forgotten usernames and passwords for your credit accounts. You will need to log into every account and gather some information. List every debt that has a balance – everything that you owe. Don't be afraid of what you might see.

Here is the good news. There is a really good chance you will feel extremely relieved once you have finished this worksheet. The fear of knowing your total amount of debt can cause you to avoid taking the steps needed to pay it off. Even if it's a large number, you will have taken the first – and often most intimidating – step to getting your debt paid.

Directions: List all of your debts and find the grand total, the number that represents your debt-free goal. Debts may include but are not limited to the following list.

- Credit card balance(s)
- Rent-to-own balance(s)
- Title loan balance(s)
- Line of credit balance(s)
- Loans (e.g. education)
- Outstanding bills (e.g. medical)
- Mortgage
- Car loan

Worksheet #2: Debt

Debt name	Balance
Credit card 1	
Credit card 2	
Credit card 3	
Loans	
Outstanding bills	
Mortgage	
Car loan	
Medical	
Student loan	
Other	
Other	
Other	
Other	
Other	
Total	

Worksheet #2 Debrief

Now you have the information needed to start paying off your debt. If this section doesn't leave you skipping and whistling through the halls, hang in there. You will use this information to create a plan that will ultimately allow you to gain control of and eliminate your debt. (We will focus on creating that plan during Step 14.)

As you make progress paying off your debt, you will enjoy watching your total debt balance drop like a rock. Watching your debt disappear is encouraging and will create motivation and a sense of accomplishment.

Mapping out your progress will keep you on track. You could be in for a long journey or a short one. It will depend on how much debt you have and how much you can afford to pay on it. You can now look forward to watching your debt shrink every time you make a payment. Every month you will get closer and closer to being free of debt, which means every month you will feel better and better about your progress.

When things can't be worse, the good news is that it can only get better. If you have debt issues, hang in there; in week three we will deal with debt head on.

Get to the root cause

What is the root cause of your debt?

Name one thing that you are doing that is helping you in your fight against debt.

_____

_____

Name two specific things that remaining in debt will prevent you from doing and having.

_____

_____

What are the results of becoming debt free?

_____

_____

_____

If you still have the same amount of debt (or more) in five years from now, would you be okay with that? Why or why not?

_____

_____

_____

What habits, choices or activities can you leave behind that will help you become debt free?

_____

_____

Celebrate your milestones

Many people are afraid to actually know their total amount of debt. In fact, this fear often holds them back from taking the important step you just took. Take a minute to realize that you are making major progress!

How does this progress feel?

_____

_____

_____

Believe that you can and will make progress. Write down your belief.

_____

_____

_____

Excellent! Keep up the momentum. Let's look at the other side of the coin.

Step 3: List Your Assets

> Worksheet Goal: Gather your assets together for a more focused picture of your financial situation.

Directions: Gather, list, and add up all of your assets. Figure out exactly how much loot you have. Include all of the liquid-ish cash assets like those suggested here.

    a. Cash
    b. Savings
    c. Checking
    d. Investments
    e. Stocks
    f. Bonds
    g. Mutual funds
    h. IRAs
    i. Value of house*

A note about the house. If you have a mortgage, you must include the market value of the house as an asset (on Worksheet #3) if you included the balance of your mortgage as a liability (Worksheet #2).

A note about your car loan. It is recommended that you include any debt on your car as a debt but do not include the value of your car as an asset. The value of your car has very little influence over your financial situation, but the balance on your car loan has great influence!

Worksheet #3: Assets

Asset name	Value
Cash	
Stocks	
Bonds	
Mutual funds	
IRA	
Value of house	
401(k)	
Other	
Other	
Other	
Other	
Other	
Total	

Worksheet #3 Debrief

Do you have a lot of assets? Great! But, what does that mean?

Assets can be used in several ways:
- Attack and eliminate debt
- Financial safety net for you and your family
- Emergency fund
- Short-term savings for purchases like cars
- Start a college fund for children
- Fund your retirement

We will determine if you have a thick enough cash cushion and a properly balanced safety net next week.

No assets? Now you know what to focus on and in what direction to travel. This worksheet might have sparked ideas for some new goals. Create some action steps to help move you closer to achieving those goals. After you complete this week's worksheets, you will have an opportunity to write down your goals and action steps.

If you have very little assets, don't get discouraged. You are taking the steps necessary to create a system that will allow you to start building more assets. Progress is close at hand.

Get to the root cause

Why do you have the amount of assets that you have?

Are your total assets healthy and appropriate for your situation? Why or why not?

_____

_____

_____

What is one thing that you are doing that is making a positive impact on your assets?

_____

_____

What is one thing that you can do better that will help you build your assets?

_____

_____

Celebrate your milestones

Whether or not you have enough assets, you have now taken another important step toward getting an accurate financial picture. Congrats!

Take a minute to write down how you see assets being useful now and in the future.

_____

_____

_____

What does saving up assets mean for you and your family?

_____

_____

What are your goals when it comes to gathering and saving assets?

_____

_____

_____

Well done! We're almost there. The next worksheet will allow you to make better sense of your debts and assets. A clear picture is moments away!

Step 4: Calculate Your Net Worth

Worksheet Goal: Pinpoint exactly where you are financially.

Directions: Pull it all together to get an idea of where you stand in your own financial "big picture." Calculate your net worth by subtracting your debts from your assets.

Worksheet #4: Assets – Debts = Net Worth

Total assets from Worksheet #3	$_____
Total debts from Worksheet #2	$_____
Net worth (Subtract the debts from the assets)	$_____

Re-figure your net worth without the mortgage (debt) and the value of the house (asset) to get a different perspective. The house and the mortgage are more or less "fixed" and aren't easily manipulated during the monthly budgeting process. You can control other areas, such as eating out or entertainment, more easily on a month-by-month basis. Unless you are planning on selling, refinancing, or paying more (or less) on your house, there isn't much to be done with it. I am not suggesting that you ignore your mortgage; just that looking at your situation from different angles can be helpful.

Worksheet #4 Debrief

Why calculate your net worth? Calculating your net worth is the best way to paint your financial big picture. Doing this boils everything down to one number, your net worth. Refiguring your net worth every quarter is the best way to track your overall progress. Your net worth is like the "you are here" sign on your financial map.

> *Your net worth is like the "you are here" sign on your financial map.*

Your net worth can also be used like a compass to guide your direction of travel. Are you getting closer to or further away from your financial goals? Your net worth will help you answer that question. When you compare this quarter's net worth to last quarter's net worth, you will clearly see the direction you are heading.

Your net worth might be a negative number. If you have a mortgage, credit cards, a car payment, and student loans, your net worth could be a very BIG negative number. Don't panic – it's that way for lots of people. It's better to know the facts about your financial situation than to remain in the dark. You need to know the facts so that you can plan accordingly. Whether your net worth is positive or negative, the rest of this workbook will point you, guide you, and move you closer to where you want to be.

Get to the root cause

Think of all the "reasons why and consequences" that your net worth represents.

Name three reasons to improve your net worth.

_____

_____

_____

Write down one challenge that will motivate you for the next four weeks to increase your net worth.

_____

_____

_____

What level of success do you expect for yourself?

_____

_____

_____

What do you need to believe about yourself in order to make these improvements?

_____

_____

_____

What is the easiest step forward you could take this week?

_____

_____

_____

Celebrate your milestones

You did it! You now have a grasp of the overall picture and you can begin to make massive progress. I'm proud of you. I bet you are starting to feel the power that this workbook holds, power that will allow you to take full control of your entire financial situation.

What does having a clear picture of your overall financial situation mean to you?

_____

_____

_____

Who can you share your accomplishment of this milestone with that will be proud and supportive of you?

_____

_____

_____

Awesome! Let's wrap it up for the week then take a much earned, deserved and needed break.

Week One Goals and Action Steps

What ideas came to mind while you were busy making all that progress? I imagine you have had lots of great ideas, asked some great questions, and thought of some great answers.

Translate those ideas into *one specific goal* you would like to accomplish for each section. Write down *one specific action step* that you can take *this week* to get closer to achieving your goal.

Worksheet 1 - Spending

Goal _____

Action step _____

Worksheet 2 - Debt

Goal _____

Action step _____

Worksheet 3 - Assets

Goal _____

Action step _____

Worksheet 4 - Net Worth

Goal _____

Action step _____

*Having goals is a good start. But taking action
is the only way to reach those goals.*

WEEK ONE SUMMARY AND CONCLUSION

What knowledge have you gained? What progress have you made? Why start here?

- We took a look at how you have been spending your money. Going through your bank statement is the most impactful thing you can do to uncover the truth and start to gain control. This exercise is part of the complete monthly budget process, located at the end of this workbook. Your bank statement history answers the questions, "Why am I here, now?" and "How did I get here?"

- We gathered information about your debts. Now you know how high the mountain is. You are now in a better place to prepare for the journey. What kind of gear do you need for the climb? How long will it take? What is the best route to travel? (We attack debt head on during week 3.)

- We gathered information about your assets. This will come into play later, while reconstructing your monthly spending habits. For example, as you make your way through the worksheets and get more focused on your goals, you might decide to use some assets to pay off a debt. Or you might want to increase the amount you save and invest each month. You'll be led through the process of making those action oriented decisions as we proceed.

- We came up with one number that says it all: your net worth. Your net worth is the "You are here" part of the map. Your net worth also works as a compass that tells you what direction you are traveling. Use this tool to make progress towards your financial goals.

- After completing these worksheets, you have a more complete picture of where you are and why. This is your starting point. Decide where you want to go and what you need to do to get there. We will fine-tune the plan for getting there in the coming weeks.

- Gathering and organizing this information is necessary to be able to make smart choices based on the facts of your situation. No more guessing.

Week one is over. Congrats and great job!

Completing all the steps is a huge step forward, *good for you*! You are taking control. If you have come this far, you are serious about getting a handle on your finances and making changes. Keep it up!

Take a break and come back for week two. Seriously, take a break. Don't burn yourself out. It takes a long time to turn a ship around. You have made major progress already. You can feel confident that you're on your way.

Download all of the audio files and listen to the recording for this week.
BeatnikBudget.com/FourWeekAudio.

Awesome. Hit me up on Twitter and let me know how it is going.
@DerekCOlsen

Week 1   Week 2   Week 3   Week 4

Week Two

WEEK TWO: ALLOCATION AND DECONSTRUCTION

Preparing to Rebuild

Introduction and goal: This week you will create healthy boundaries, set appropriate spending levels, deconstruct the parts that aren't working well, and push the reset button on your spending habits.

You will clarify what your liquid assets represent. Then you will create and implement systems that will protect your money from yourself and from others. After you have those important pieces in place, we will identify expenses you can easily do without. Once that step is complete, you will define what your true values are and make sure your decisions are supported by your values. And of course we will make sure that your decisions are bringing you closer to your goals. You will then be able to press the reset button on your spending habits, officially taking the first step towards a new plan that will work better.

Last week you found out where you are and what you have to work with. Does your current situation match where you want to be and what you want to have? If not, what needs to change? What parts are you going to keep the same? What parts are you going to throw out the window and leave behind? What parts would you like to keep because they are working well? What new methods would you like to add to your financial plan?

These are some questions that we will answer this week.

Step 5: Allocate Your Cash Savings

> ## Worksheet Goal: Properly build and allocate your cash savings.

If you have cash in the bank, what is it doing for you? Do you have a plan for your cash? If you lost your job today, how long could you stay above water without an income? Do you have enough cash saved up for major purchases like a new car, the holidays, vacations and medical expenses?

Consider this example: Say you have $1,800 in a checking account and $2,200 in savings. There are several ways to allocate those funds across the different categories. And all of the categories should have a cash reserve. Let's find out what that $4,000 truly represents. Give each dollar a name while it sits in savings so that you can get an accurate read on what that money can do for you.

Spread too thin: (Not covered properly.)	Spread properly: (Didn't go very far, did it?)
$4,000	$4,000
$1,000 - Four months' expenses	$4,000 ≈ One month's expenses
$1,000 - Emergency	$0 - Emergency
$400 - Car replacement	$0 - Car replacement
$500 - Annual insurance	$0 - Annual insurance
$300 - Vacation	$0 - Vacation
$100 - Clothing	$0 - Clothing
$200 - Holidays	$0 - Holidays
$300 - Medical	$0 - Medical
$200 - Housing	$0 - Housing
= Zero left over, fully allocated	**= Zero left over, fully allocated**

While $4,000 may sound like a lot of money, it won't cover the first savings category for most people. For most it would only last a few weeks. The sum of $4,000 might be more than you have, or it might be pocket change. Either way, please don't let the numbers used in this example weaken the concept.

Avoid the danger of mentally spending all of your savings three or four times. It is a strange trick that our minds can play. It is fairly common to mistakenly think the money will go three or four times further than it can. Look at the examples below for an illustration.

$4,000 "mentally spent" 7 times	This looks better
$4,000	$28,000 (Cash in the bank)
$15,000 - Four months' expenses	$15,000 - Four months' expenses
$2,000 - Emergency	$2,000 - Emergency
$5,000 - Car replacement	$5,000 - Car replacement
$500 - Annual insurance	$500 - Annual insurance
$2,000 - Vacation	$2,000 - Vacation
$500 - Clothing	$500 - Clothing
$1,000 - Holidays	$1,000 - Holidays
$1,000 - Medical	$1,000 - Medical
$1,000 - Housing	$1,000 - Housing
= $24,000 OVER	**= Zero left over, fully allocated**

It takes closer to $28,000 to cover everything properly for the average person - *seven times the original savings amount* used in this example.

Worksheet #5: What Is My Cash Savings For?

Directions: Take your current total cash savings (checking and savings) and divvy it up. Put every dollar you have into a category. Give your cash savings a more tangible and intentional meaning. (Cash only: no stocks, bonds, mutual funds, investments, or IRAs.)

Total cash savings	$
Emergency fund	$
Four months' expenses	$
Car replacement	$
Insurance	$
Medical	$
Clothing	$
Vacation	$
Holidays	$
Household	$
Other	$
Other	$
Total	**Zero left over, fully allocated**

Worksheet #5 Debrief

What is your cash doing for you? How far did your cash go? If it covered everything, great! If not, what do you need to re-think? Think of some goals and actions that will help get you closer to where you want to be.

> *Holidays, new cars, and vacations are coming; plan for them.*

Most of the expenses used in this example are to be expected. Holidays, new cars, and vacations are coming; plan for them. It's also important to plan for the unexpected by setting up a properly funded emergency fund. Unexpected things WILL happen, plan for them now.

There are clear steps you can take if your cash won't cover everything properly. Rather than spread your cash too thin over all the categories, consider the following plan.

- Start filling each category, from top to bottom as they are listed. Fill them up, one by one, category by category. For example, start by allotting a certain monthly amount to the emergency fund.
- When the emergency fund is full, move on to four months' expenses. Once that second category is full, move on to the next, and so on.
- Only add money to the category you are funding, filling each of them one at a time. This could mean hand-made Christmas gifts for a year or two, no vacations until the car fund is full, or no new household items until medical is covered. Each time a trade-off like this comes up, keep in mind that it's only temporary. Make sacrifices now and your future will be a much better place to live. Staying home from vacation for two years in order to avoid having a car payment for the rest of your life is a smart idea. Doing this will help you reach your long-term goals.

Maybe you are wondering how much you should have in each category. Experts advise you start with three to six months of expenses - let's use the example of four months. How much does it cost you to live for four months? Calculate all of your monthly living expenses. Refer to your work in Worksheet #1 and make sure to include rent, bills, gas, utilities, food, travel…everything. Your emergency fund should be roughly 15 percent of your four months' expenses. Next, calculate a realistic number for the remaining categories.

The bonus savings worksheet on page 106 will help you create a plan to save for each category. You can also find it at BeatnikBudget.com/Bonus.

Get to the root cause

Ask yourself those two questions again: "Why do I have this much (or little) money saved?" and "What are the positive and negative consequences of having this much cash saved up?" Get to the root cause so that you can identify what work needs to be done. Come up with some ideas for improvement, and then put them to work for you as soon as possible.

Name one savings category that you could work on funding better.

_____

_____

_____

What is one concern you have about your savings, and how can you overcome it?

_____

_____

_____

What is one area that you are ignoring that you can begin to address this week?

_____

_____

_____

How will these changes help you reach your savings goals?

_____

_____

_____

Celebrate your milestones

You now have a handle on how to manage your cash savings, and you've experienced a reality check on just how far your savings will go.

How does being aware of changes you need to make to build an adequate cash savings prepare you for the rest of your financial turnaround?

_____

_____

_____

What does your cash savings vision look like, and how does it motivate you to move forward?

_____

_____

_____

This is valuable information that will allow you to make smart choices. Those smart choices will get you closer and closer to your financial goals.

Excellent work! Let's talk a little more about cash and what it can do for you.

Step 6: Create a Cash Only System

> # Worksheet Goal: Create healthy spending boundaries using a cash only system.

It is up to you to put a cap on the amount of money you spend each month. Believe it or not, you are the one who chooses how much you spend each month and on what. There are thousands of people who want you to spend your money rather then keep it and maybe a handful of people who would rather you keep it than spend it. The overwhelming influence in the world is attempting to get you to spend your money. It is up to you to provide reasons and decide to save. With so many influences tempting you to spend your money in various ways, it is hard to go against the grain and make the decision to be responsible with it. Using a cash only system is the most powerful way to make sure you stay in control of how much you spend.

There are three reasons to use a cash only system: emotional, accounting, and time.

Emotional: When you use cash instead of credit cards, you feel the impact of the purchase immediately – that money is gone, forever. You will also be intimately aware of how much you have available to spend. Creating an emotional connection to your spending habits is a great way to establish a healthy relationship with your money.

Accounting: How much did you spend last month on groceries, restaurant meals, lunches, coffee and snacks, drinks, and entertainment? It's not that easy to recall off the top of your head, is it? With a properly kept cash system, however, it's incredibly easy. Just take the amount you started with and subtract what is left. This method makes accounting a breeze.

Time: Going through your bank statement takes time. Making just four cash only categories (grocery/store, restaurant, entertainment, and his/hers) will drastically reduce the amount of time it takes to reconcile your budget later. Doing this will replace 20 or 30 lines on your bank statement with one cash withdrawal. Easy!

A cash only system will replace 20 or 30 lines on your bank statement with one cash withdrawal. Easy!

The Cash Only System Explained:

1. Decide what categories will become cash only categories. For this example we will use the following:
   a. Grocery or "store"*
   b. Restaurant
   c. Entertainment
   d. His & hers discretionary cash

2. Decide how much cash you need for each cash category. For this example we will allot $600 to store, $120 to restaurant, $100 to entertainment and $100 for his/hers ($50 each) = $920 total.

3. Withdraw $920 from the bank. (TIP: Some prefer to take half out on the 1st and the other half on the 15th.) Grab some envelopes, jars, paperclips, or whatever you will use to keep the cash separated. A coupon holder works well too.

4. Use Worksheet #6 to note the amounts for each category each month. Keep the worksheet in the same location as the cash.

5. When you are at the store, use the cash from the store envelope. When you go out to lunch or dinner, use the cash from the restaurant envelope, and so on. When the money runs out, you are finished for the month. Don't go get more cash or use your credit card. Don't borrow from the other envelopes either.

Create a new cash category for any area that needs to be watched closely. Perhaps a cash category for gasoline or a hobby of yours might be helpful.

Paying cash only takes some planning, practice, and patience. But once you set up the system, you will begin to experience the power of using it. And you will love the results.

---

*"Store" includes small household items like toothpaste and dish soap. It works the same regardless of whether you decide to split the store category into food and non-food. Try these two methods to see what works best: First, label food and small household items as the store category. Next, try splitting it up between food and household items. Use whichever way serves you best. Results are what we are looking for. The method you use can vary.

Worksheet #6: The Cash Only System

Directions: Create your own cash only system.

Month/Year _____

Category	Start amount	End amount	Leftover amount
Grocery/store			
Restaurant			
Entertainment			
His			
Hers			
Other			
Other			
Total			

Worksheet #6 Debrief

This is an auto-correcting system; it will balance itself out every month. If you take out $920 and have $60 left over at the end of the month, only withdraw $860 for next month. This will build your cash back up to $920. In other words, begin each month with the same starting total. This helps train you to spend a consistent monthly amount. The result will be spending habits that help you get closer to your goals.

One more thing: Let's say you drive all the way to the store and realize you forgot the cash. Drive all the way back home and get it. You will only have to do this once. You won't forget again.

Make it fun. Make it work. The results are worth it.

Get to the root cause

What are the "whys" and positive and negative consequences of using (or not using) a cash only system?

Name two ways that a cash only system can help you.

_____

_____

_____

Name two specific things that a cash only system will allow you to do or have.

_____

_____

_____

What other healthy limitations have you placed on your spending that are working well?

_____

_____

_____

Celebrate your milestones

You have now created a system that makes you very aware of your spending. When you are aware, you can be more in control.

How will a cash only system help you feel more in charge and organized?

_____

_____

Way to go! You're getting there. Feeling good, right? Me too! The next worksheet is one of my favorites. This one will produce instant results.

Step 7: Unplug

> ### Worksheet Goal: Create instant progress by canceling monthly subscriptions.

A great way to make an immediate impact on next month's budget is to cancel several monthly subscription services. You will see immediate results from following this plan. Some of these subscription services aren't even good for us.

They could be:

- Unhealthy
- A poor use of time
- Not worth the money
- Unnecessary
- Easily replaced with other free or cheaper alternatives

Here is the part that gets most people. Before you claim to have nothing you can cancel, carefully think about everything on this list.

Take a minute to honestly evaluate how (and why) you are using these services. If you use them, get your money's worth, and can afford them, spend on! But just because you can afford something does not mean you have to buy it. Think about all the other things you could do with that money. Think about it in those terms and then make your decision to keep or cancel.

Subscriptions to consider:

1. Cable TV
2. Internet service
3. Cable/TV/phone bundle packages
4. Magazine and newspaper subscriptions
5. Alumni association
6. Gym membership
7. Unnecessary online computer protection
8. Water treatment equipment service
9. Auto-renewing warranties and memberships
10. Online music and movie subscriptions
11. Excessive text messaging payment plan
12. Excessive cell phone data plan
13. Club and group membership dues
14. Home phone service
15. Cell phone service
16. Any service that charges you on a recurring basis
17. Storage unit payment
18. Home security system
19. Timeshare rights
20. Find your own thing to get rid of

Directions: Write down all of your monthly bills, recurring payments, memberships, and subscriptions. List only the things that you have to actually cancel – by phone, email, or snail mail - in order to be rid of it. Make sure to list ALL of them. If you decide to keep one, write *keep* under the action column. Otherwise, write down the action needed to cancel the account and then fill in the date you took that action.

Worksheet #7: Unplug

Item	Cost	Action	Date unplugged
EXAMPLE: Cable TV	$85	Call cable company	5/3/2014
Total			

Worksheet #7 Debrief

What else could you do with the monthly savings?

_____

_____

Your answers above can easily be thought of as goals and action steps.

Example: Because I canceled my cable bill, I can afford to save $85 more a month or put $85 more towards my car payment.

Make sure that you have a plan in place for every dollar that you are able to free up. The redirecting of each dollar should be intentional, carefully considered, and then completed with proper follow-through. Don't let that extra $85 get away!

Get to the root cause

Dig deep into the "whys" on this worksheet. Ask yourself what these services and subscriptions mean to you.

Do you have too many subscriptions that are slowing you down? Please explain.

_____

_____

_____

Are they worth the cost? Please explain.

_____

_____

_____

Do you really want and need them? Please explain.

_____

_____

_____

Name two specific subscriptions that you could do without for the next two years.

_____

_____

Do you believe that doing without them could help you feel better about your finances? Please explain.

_____

_____

Celebrate your milestones

When we get used to subscriptions and memberships we start spending our money on "autopilot," rather than deliberately.

What does it feel like to carefully consider all the options for your spending?

_____

_____

_____

How can stepping out of your comfort zone allow you to make progress?

_____

_____

_____

Write a quick note to yourself celebrating the fact that you are making meaningful progress.

_____

_____

_____

Nice job! You are looking good. Let's keep it up. Let's take a different look at some of your spending.

Step 8: Just STOP!

> ### Worksheet Goal: Redirect even more cash by carefully considering impulse purchases.

STOP! DON'T! QUIT!

Whatever you have to say to yourself, just don't do it.

Let's focus on the expenses that are not subscriptions, but that you still have control over – the impulse buys.

These purchases are often hard to identify. They don't show up as a bill in the mail. They are silent killers that add up little by little over the days, weeks, months, and years. Going unchecked, just one of these can cause big trouble.

If you received a bill at the end of the month from 7-Eleven for $120, Quickie Mart for $87, and Starbucks for $113, what would you do? Would you get angry and call them up right away to dispute the false bill? I would. But they would turn right around and respond by providing a record of the facts, proving beyond a doubt that you do in fact owe them. (Maybe showing you on video, day in and day out, making all those impulse buys!) You could only get mad at and blame yourself, not them. This is another reason why we do the bank statement exercise each month. It's the only way to see these small purchases added up together. We often don't notice them for what they truly are otherwise.

Things would be different if convenience stores sent their customers a bill at the end of the month instead of charging at the time of purchase. Those smaller amounts are easier to absorb. All the spending adds up unnoticed.

Worksheet #8: STOP IT!

Directions: Write down all the small purchases you make on a daily and weekly basis - purchases that you can easily eliminate, cut in half, or replace with something much less expensive or free. Refer back to your bank statement for ideas if necessary.

Item	Eliminate Y/N	Cut back?	Replace with	Amount saved
EXAMPLE: Coffee	No	Yes	Home brewed coffee	$2 a day/$40 a month
Monthly amount saved				

Worksheet #8 Debrief

What else could you do with the money saved?

_____

_____

_____

Example: Because I stopped buying a candy bar, soda and lottery ticket every day I can afford to start investing $170 more a month or put $170 more towards paying off my student loan.

Have a plan in place for every dollar that you are able to free up. The redirecting of this money should be intentional, with a specific plan for each dollar. Don't let that extra $170 slip through *your* fingers!

Beware of little expenses;
a small leak will sink a great ship.
-Ben Franklin

Get to the root cause

Impulse buys happen when your mind is furthest away from the root cause. An impulse buy is the opposite of asking, "Why?" An impulse buy is completely void of any thought about future consequences. Dig deep again on this section.

Why is it important for your overall financial situation to pay close attention to impulse buys?

_____

_____

_____

What do you need to continually tell yourself in order to limit your impulse buys?

_____

_____

_____

Name a time that you passed up an impulse buy. Recall the circumstances and reasons that allowed you to make that decision.

_____

_____

_____

How will limiting your impulse buys help you move forward financially?

_____

_____

_____

Celebrate your milestones

Impulse spending adds up fast and often goes unnoticed.

The feeling of control that you get when you refuse to make an impulse buy can translate to many other areas of life. In what other areas do you regularly exercise self-control?

_____

_____

_____

How can you reward yourself each time you pass up on an impulse buy?

_____

_____

_____

Recall the example in the introduction about the chain reaction of staying up too late, not having enough time to get ready, then having to stop and buy coffee. Getting to the root cause of your impulse buying is crucial for creating changes that will last. Uncover the reasons why you make impulse buys and deal with the root cause, don't just deny yourself the purchase. That will just leave you frustrated. Address the root cause, and consider the positive things you could do with that money.

Looking good! Let's continue.

The next worksheet is consistently voted most helpful by those who attend my workshops.

BeatnikBudget.com/Workshops.

But first, check out the 25/24 rule on the next page.

Bonus: The 25/24 Rule

If it costs more than $25, wait 24 hours.

Twice a week or more we are tempted by an impulse buy that is between $25 and $100. A purchase that you "can afford." You have the money in your account, but that doesn't actually mean you can afford it. And even if you *can* afford it, that doesn't mean you need it, have to buy it, or should buy it. If you practice the 24/25 rule, resisting those impulse buys will get easier and it will pay off.

Ways of exercising the 24/25 rule include but are not limited to:

- *Sleep on it:* Acting in the moment has gotten lots of people in trouble. Lots of dumb decisions have been made in the moment without thinking. I've made a few, how about you? How many mistakes would never have been made if cooler heads where allowed to prevail? Waiting a full day will give your emotions a chance to reset. When you wait a full day, you are no longer acting on pure emotion. There are chemicals that affect the human brain's decision making process. Fortunately, they flush out in a matter of minutes, allowing the real you to regain control over your decisions.
- *Think about it:* An impulse buy is just that: NOT thinking about it. Stepping back for a day will allow you to think about the purchase from multiple angles. You might end up realizing that you don't really need or even want the item. This time will allow you to think of the big picture and the outcome, not just the impulse purchase in question.
- *Talk about it with others:* Over the course of a full day you can talk about it with a few people and get their opinion. Get mine: Derek@BeatnikBudget.com. (Spoiler alert, I will tell you not to buy it!)

Avoid buyer's remorse. I've been there and done that. I bought a yearlong gym membership once for hundreds of dollars. I knew the second I bought it that it was a mistake. I went to that gym about 12 times during the first two months and then never went back. That sucks. It's very hard to experience buyer's remorse over buying something that was well planned and thought out. But it's even harder when you regret making the purchase! That gym tried to charge my card again a year later as a convenience. That sucked even more.

It will get easier and easier to resist impulse buys. Keep in mind the reasons for limiting them and the more advantageous ways that you could spend that money.

Bottom line: The money stays in your pocket.

Step 9: Is This Appropriate?

> ## Worksheet Goal: Align your spending habits to properly reflect your values, needs and goals.

Actions speak louder than words

Is the way you spend your money appropriate when considering your values, wants and needs, and goals? Proper alignment will get you closer to achieving your goals.

Consider each spending category in order from most to least expensive. Then, compare the position of each individual category in relation to all the other categories' positions. Last, ask the following question:

> *Is the amount of money I spend on this item appropriate?*

When you ask yourself this question, consider the item and its cost in two ways:

> Consideration one: *Is the amount of money I spend on this item appropriate in comparison to the amount of money I spend on other items?*

For example, "Is it appropriate to spend more on golf than on my retirement account?" The answer to this question will depend on several factors. Your values, priorities, wants, needs, stage of life, overall financial profile, and other personal factors of your own. The answer to this example question could be, *"Yes, it is appropriate to spend more on golf than on my retirement account each month because I am 70 years old, I have already fully funded my retirement accounts, and I enjoy golfing away my golden years."* Or, *"No, it is not appropriate because I am 27 years old, I am not saving as much as I need to, and my life would be just fine without golf."*

Another example goes like this. Let's say that you are spending four times more each month on your rent then you are spending on your children. Based on all the criteria you may conclude that *this is indeed appropriate.* Don't let the fact that you are spending more on an item that you don't value as highly as another wrongly affect your answer. It is very possible to correctly and appropriately spend less money on something that you value very much (like your children) in comparison to something that you value less (like your house).

Consideration two: *Is the amount of money I spend on this item appropriate without considering the amount of money I spend on other items?*

Simply because you spend less on golf in comparison to your retirement account does not mean that each category is balanced appropriately. You might come to the conclusion that each category needs adjustment, independent of the relationship between the two. For example, it's great if you're spending less on golf than retirement. But don't stop there. Consider the amount you're spending on golf each month independent of its relativity to other expenses and ask yourself if it is appropriate for you when considering your values and goals.

Directions:

1. Record the monthly amount spent on each category.
2. Rank each category from highest to lowest cost (1 = most expensive).
3. Compare each category to the other categories and ask the two questions provided in the previous section.
   a. *Is the amount of money I spend on this item appropriate when considering the amount of money I spend on other items?* Yes or no?
   b. *Is the amount of money I spend on this item appropriate without considering the amount of money I spend on other items?* Yes or no?
4. List your answers (yes or no) on the following worksheet (9a).

Worksheet #9a: Is This Appropriate?

Item	Monthly Cost	Rank from most to least expensive. (1-21)	Appropriate when compared to others? (Y/N)	Appropriate independent of others? (Y/N)
Rent or mortgage				
All monthly bills				
Car payment				
Loan payment				
Credit cards				
All other debt				
Groceries				
Eating out				
Clothing				
Car – gasoline				
Car – maintenance				
Entertainment				
Alcohol/cigarettes/vices				
Children/family				
Vacation/travel				
Medical				
Savings				
Giving				
Investing				
Insurance				
All other/mystery				

Worksheet #9b: Appropriate Changes

Directions: Write down the spending categories that you have decided aren't being considered appropriately. What areas aren't in alignment with your values and your goals? Write the change to be made and the reason for making that change in the corresponding column. This will uncover the places where you can improve your spending patterns.

Inappropriate category	Change to be made	Reason why
EXAMPLE: "Retirement"	Start saving $100 more each month	Secure future that I feel good about

Worksheet #9 Debrief

This exercise allows you to view your spending through the lens of appropriateness. There are two different lenses. Comparing between spending categories and comparison within each category independent of the others.

When you consider your values, priorities, and goals you get to determine the appropriateness of your spending in each category. Consider all the factors that are important to you when you start to make changes. Carefully think about why you are making these changes.

Consider this illustration: As a bricklayer builds a house, s/he must put each brick in its correct place in relation to all the other bricks and must also pay attention to each brick alone. Without knowing it, the bricklayer asks the two questions, "Is this brick appropriate when considering the whole job?" and, "Is this brick appropriate for this specific location within the job?"

Here is a quick and easy guideline for making changes:

- Decide on your goals
- Determine where you are now
- Identify the discrepancies between where you are and where you want to be
- Discover what needs to change
- Decide how to make those changes happen
- Take action

In other words:

- Where am I now?
- Where do I want to be?
- How am I going to get there?

Get to the root cause

How will this new awareness help you in your progress? Answering a few questions at this point in the process is super helpful.

What is one spending category that you determined is out of sync with your values?

_____

_____

_____

How can you make an adjustment to align that category with your values?

_____

_____

_____

What is a spending category that is in sync with your values?

_____

_____

_____

Celebrate your milestones

This exercise can be very revealing – especially when you see that there is a discrepancy between the path that you are on and the destination you wish to arrive at.

Explain how this step helped bring more clarity to your vision of financial peace of mind.

_____

_____

_____

How will aligning your spending habits with your values help move you closer to your goals?

_____

_____

_____

Who can you share your successes with that will be proud of you and celebrate your progress with you?

_____

_____

_____

Send them a quick email or text telling them about your progress!

Nicely done! You're getting there. Just one more worksheet this week.

Now is your chance to make some real, tangible changes.

Step 10: Where did it go? Where should it go?

> ## Worksheet Goal: Press the reset button and reallocate your money based on the results you want.

Create a practice budget

Directions:

PART 1: Actual

Go through last month's bank statement and put every expenditure into one of the categories. Use a scratch sheet of paper to keep a running total of each category. To stay organized, place a checkmark on the bank statement next to each line as you add it to the correct category on the scratch sheet of paper. Add up all the running subtotals to get a total for each category. Write that number on the worksheet below in the ACTUAL column. You want to discover how you actually spent your money last month. Give names to the generic categories on Worksheet #10. Add new categories if you need to.

PART 2: Budgeted

Take charge of your money and tell it where to go and what to do. Fill out the budgeted column with how you plan to spend your money this month. For example, if you reduce restaurant spending by $200, you could increase your savings by $200 or increase the amount that you put towards paying off debt by $200. These new numbers go into the BUDGETED column. For every dollar you decrease in any category, you get to increase another category that same amount. Consider everything that we have covered so far while you create your new plan. Move closer to your goals. This part will feel amazing!

PART 3: Difference

Calculate the difference between the BUDGETED column and the ACTUAL column. For the spending categories, you will subtract the actual amounts from the budgeted amounts. On the income line, you will subtract the budgeted from the actuals. The differences represent changes that you need to make in your spending habits throughout the month. The DIFFERENCE column reveals your goals and action items. Then subtract your total spending from your income to find the total left over.

Worksheet #10: Preliminary Budget

Month/Year_____			
Item	Budgeted	- Actual	= Difference
Income			
Giving			
Cash withdrawal			
Rent / mortgage			
Bill #1			
Bill #2			
Bill #3			
Bill #4			
Bill #5			
Bill #6			
Cell phone			
Grocery			
Restaurant			
Car insurance			
*Emergency fund			
*4 months' expenses			
*Car replacement			
*Insurance			
*Medical			
*Holidays			
*Clothing			
*Vacation / travel			
*Household items			
Debt #1			
Debt #2			

Debt #3			
Student loan			
Car: gas / oil / repair			
Entertainment			
Gifts			
Investing / retirement			
Hobby			
Alcohol / cigs			
Other			
Other			
Other			
Unexpected # 1			
Unexpected # 2			
Unexpected # 3			
Total income			
Total spending			
Subtract total income from total spending (should equal zero)			

*These categories represent savings.

If you end up having left over money, distribute it into your savings categories. Remember that the purpose of this worksheet is to identify the difference between what you actually spent last month and how you would like to spend your money this month so that you can make spending and/or budgeting adjustments. Again, make sure you subtracted the budgeted from the actual on the income line only.

The savings categories are explained in more detail on the BONUS worksheet on page 106.

Worksheet #10 Debrief

How did it go? Are you ready to put your new plan into practice?

Economics is the study of how *limited resources* are allocated. At any given time, you only have so much money. It is not unlimited. Most personal financial troubles stem from simply spending more than was earned. Every dollar spent here is a dollar that you can't spend anywhere else. You get to choose where every dollar goes; each dollar can only go one place, one time. Choose wisely when you allocate your limited resources.

If you need another dollar "here," it has to come from a "there." It is wise to intentionally identify what the "here" and the "there" actually are. Give them both a name, something that is real. *$200 less on shopping = $200 more towards your emergency fund.* Identify something that is tangible. Don't just wish that you had another $100. Money is just a representative for something real, like shopping or cable TV. Every dollar has an equal.

The information in this exercise is very powerful. You can begin to turn the financial tide by creating a plan based on your current situation, your desired situation, and the difference between the two. This exercise allows you to paint a picture of what you want your monthly budget to look like. Imagine a future where your money does what *you* want it to. You can achieve that future by using this worksheet as a goal generation tool. Let it point you toward your ideal financial goal – a sustainable monthly budget that you control. This is your chance to dig up those bad roots and plant healthy ones. Healthy roots will produce the healthy results you want.

Your new plan must be a balance between your goals and what you can realistically achieve. Being realistic is key. Some people get excited at this point and set unrealistic goals that aren't achievable, given their current situation. Then when they experience a "failure," they get frustrated and sometimes blame the process and claim that it doesn't work. The fact is they may have set unrealistic goals and set themselves up for failure from the very beginning. Don't let this happen to you, be realistic and find the balance.

Get to the root cause

Name one specific reason why there is a difference between the way you are spending your money and the way you would like to be spending your money.

_____

_____

_____

Name one category of spending that you are managing well.

_____

_____

_____

How can you apply what you are doing well to the other categories?

_____

_____

_____

How will you alter your spending habits and other decisions now that you have identified which areas need the most work?

_____

_____

_____

Celebrate your milestones

A preliminary budget is a *major* milestone along your journey. Hitting the reset button and starting over allows you to leave behind the parts that aren't working and add some new parts that will work better. Now is your chance to hit the restart button. This is a great place to start moving in a new direction.

What excites you the most about putting a new budgeting plan into practice?

_____

_____

_____

How does it feel to know that you have taken just a few more steps in the right direction?

_____

_____

_____

Who can you share your excitement with? We all need people to help us celebrate; send someone who will support and celebrate with you a text or an email!

Keep in mind the big picture. Remember, you aren't just moving numbers around on a spreadsheet. You have a vision. You have a goal. Keep your reasons in mind while you have your head buried in the details.

Brilliant! Let's wrap things up for the week and get ready for another break.

Week Two Goals and Action Steps

Before we stop for the week, think about what ideas came to mind while you were making progress. I imagine you have had lots of great ideas, asked some great questions, and thought of some great answers. Translate those ideas into *one specific goal* you would like to accomplish. Then write down *one specific action step* that you can take *this week* to get closer to achieving that goal.

Worksheet 5 – Cash savings

Goal _____

Action step _____

Worksheet 6 – Cash only

Goal _____

Action step _____

Worksheet 7 – Unplugging

Goal _____

Action step _____

Worksheet 8 – Impulse

Goal _____

Action step _____

Worksheet 9 – Appropriate

Goal _____

Action step _____

Worksheet 10 – Monthly budget

Goal _____

Action step _____

WEEK TWO SUMMARY AND CONCLUSION

What have you uncovered this week? How will this help?

- We identified the value of having clear boundaries for cash. With this information you were able to set up a structure that will help stabilize your saving and spending.

- We discussed ways to take control of our savings by labeling what the cash savings is earmarked for. Next, we created a cash only system to establish healthy boundaries between you and your money.

- We started deconstructing spending habits and then identified unnecessary monthly expenses. These included recurring subscriptions and impulse buys. Examining the reasons behind those purchases helped you make clear decisions.

- We worked through a process to clarify and prioritize your values and then created a plan of action that will better reflect those values. This way, your new spending habits will lead you toward your desired future.

- We created a practice budget, which helped you uncover tangible changes you can make to your spending habits.

- Our work this week put you into a position to hit the reset and restart buttons. This gives you the chance to leave behind the parts that aren't working and replace them with parts that will work better.

Remember to always ask why. Why do you spend your money this way? Make sure to explore the positive and negative consequences of each action. There is always an immediate and a future outcome to every decision you make. Make sure the outcome is what you really want. Keep the big picture and your goals in mind. There are deeper reasons behind rearranging numbers on a spreadsheet. Those numbers have a real-world application and meaning.

Week two is over. Congrats and great job!

Listen to the audio for week two: BeatnikBudget.com/FourWeekAudio.

~~Week 1~~   ~~Week 2~~   Week 3   Week 4

Week Three

WEEK THREE: JUMP START AND RECONSTRUCTION

Re-wire your pocketbook. Get a jumpstart. Take action.

Introduction and goal: This week is all about reconstruction. Now that you have deconstructed some of the habits and structures that weren't working well, we will begin to replace the broken parts with new parts that work better.

You already hit the restart button so let's get started!

You will learn how to de-clutter and simplify things so that you can stay on track and be focused, effective, and efficient. You'll be able to find ways to earn extra cash by selling some stuff and/or earning extra income.

As we conclude for the week, you'll devise a plan to attack debt. You'll also learn how to define your wants versus your needs. We will talk in terms of survival, maintenance, and thriving. You will get an understanding of the magic behind automatic payments, savings, and investing and then learn how to set up a system like this for yourself.

Let's start the reconstruction process.

Step 11: Sell It for Cash

> ## Worksheet Goal: Jump-start your financial turnaround with quick cash.

You might have some cash sitting around in your garage or basement. Cash that could be doing much more than just collecting dust and taking up space. By selling a few items and making some quick cash, you can jump-start your progress toward your financial turnaround. You can create instant success while de-cluttering your house at the same time.

This is often the point when people get excited about taking action. There is something magical about cleaning house and selling stuff. It can really get the blood pumping. The physical action and the real, cash-money rewards lead to an emotional boost as well. This feeling of success is transferrable to the other areas of this process. You are excited, I can tell.

Pick out a few things to sell, sell them, and enjoy the feeling of success. Transfer that feeling (and that cash) to the rest of your financial turnaround.

Check out this blog post about how we made $156 an hour at our garage sale. There are lots of great tips in there for getting the most out of your efforts, and junk.

BeatnikBudget.com/GarageSale.

Worksheet #11: Sell It for Cash

Directions: List all the major items you could sell. Determine what the total dollar amount might be. Daydream about what you could do with that cash. Then take action.

Item	Asking Price	Date Sold	Actual Price
Boat	$7000	7-7-2014	$6500
Total			

Worksheet #11 Debrief

What could you do with the money earned in step #11? Don't let that money get away from you. Could you pay off a debt? Start a retirement account? Build up cash savings for an emergency fund? EXAMPLE: Because I sold my boat, I can pay off my car!

With the money earned, I can

_____

_____

_____

Get to the root cause

What does cleaning house and making some extra cash feel like?

_____

_____

_____

How will this project help reduce your stress and give you momentum?

_____

_____

_____

What is your biggest challenge when it comes to de-cluttering, and how can you overcome it?

_____

_____

_____

Celebrate your milestones

When you de-clutter you can free up cash that can be put toward higher value uses. When you consider selling each item, ask yourself why you still own each item and what else you could do with the money earned from selling it.

Write a quick note to yourself explaining how this step is important for your financial future.

_____

_____

_____

_____

What will you do with the cash that you earn from taking this step?

_____

_____

_____

How can you use this momentum to make even more progress this week?

_____

_____

_____

Very good! Now let's get even more cash for you.

Step 12: Extra Income

> Worksheet Goal: Put your income on high speed so you can make progress even faster.

You might have to dig in further and do some extra, real work. Even if you already have a job, you can do something else in your off time that can bring in extra cash. Maybe you can work an extra shift or take a side job – whatever you need to do to make the tide turn in your favor.

Once you have earned a pre-determined amount of money from the extra job and your financial situation is heading in the right direction, you can quit the second job.

Visit the bonus webpage for a list of side-job ideas. BeatnikBudget.com/Bonus.

Worksheet #12: Extra Income

Directions: List potential jobs you could do to earn some extra cash. Extra cash that will help you reduce your debt or build savings more quickly.

Extra job	Pay	Quit when:
EXAMPLE: Mowing lawns	*$30/lawn*	*Car is paid off ($2,000)*
EXAMPLE: Paper delivery	*$50/day*	*Emergency fund is full ($1,200)*

Worksheet #12 Debrief

Whistle while you work away that debt and smile as you save for retirement.

The ultimate debt-destruction double threat: reducing your spending while increasing your income. It's a lot like losing weight using the most powerful technique possible – increasing the exercise AND eating healthier. When you use both techniques at the same time, you accomplish your goal much faster than if you use just one technique by itself.

Keep in mind that this is a temporary situation to help get your finances to a better place. While you are working this extra job, think of the goal, not the job. Doing so will help pass the time and help you enjoy the extra work more. The knowledge that this extra work has a specific result will encourage you to stick with it. After you achieve your goal, feel free to quit. Your reason for doing the extra work no longer exists.

This is not a punishment, something to be embarrassed by, or a step backwards. You are committed to success and you are willing to do whatever it takes to turn your finances around. Dedicated people like you are willing to roll up their sleeves and get a little dirty. Don't worry about what others might think. You are making smart choices and serious progress.

I suggest doing the extra work for a short time only, just to get to a more stable place financially. Doing this extra work is usually not a long-term sustainable plan and it doesn't have to be. In fact, you shouldn't have to work a double shift to *stay* above water, but perhaps only to *get* above water. The goal is to then arrange your financial situation in such a way that you can stay afloat without the extra work.

Think of your big picture goals and remember that this extra work is for a reason, and temporary.

Get to the root cause

- -

Can you seriously consider taking on some extra work as part of your financial turnaround plan?

_____

_____

_____

What frustrations or concerns do you have regarding getting another job? How can you overcome them?

_____

_____

_____

What are the results of doing and not doing extra work?

_____

_____

_____

Your efforts will have a compound effect when you work both sides of the financial turnaround equation.

What was that equation again? Income – Spending = Your Financial Situation

How about: Earning Money + Choices = Current Situation

Or as my friend Kent Julian says: Events + Your Response = Outcome

Remember to attach a specific goal or "why" to any (temporary) extra work you do. Think of the positive consequences and results attached to the extra work. "Why am I going to work on Saturday?" "Oh yeah, to pay off my car, and that is going to feel awesome!"

Celebrate your milestones

How does the extra work that you are doing reflect your belief that your financial turnaround will be successful?

_____

_____

_____

How will it feel to make noticeable progress by doing extra work?

_____

_____

_____

Good work! Now let's talk about freedom from debt. Becoming debt free is the single most important part of your financial journey!

Step 13: Debt, the Worst Four-Letter Word

> Worksheet Goal: Organize your debt payment plan and move closer to a debt free lifestyle.

There are entire bookstore sections devoted to getting out of debt. Those shelves are filled with many excellent theories on the subject.

But for our purposes, we don't need to go into theory. This next worksheet will help you stay in focused action in order to reduce your debt as quickly as possible. When it comes to working your way out of debt, it's all about action, action, action. Theory is great, but the bottom line is throwing as many dollars as fast as you can at your debt.

It may feel a bit uncomfortable to gather all of this information into one place. You might be worried about seeing the total amount, once you add everything together. Some people treat debt as "out of sight, out of mind." But that's not for you. Face your debt head on!

Remember Step 5 when we talked about how we "mentally spend" three or four times the actual value of cash on hand? Our minds do the opposite when it comes to debt. We can compartmentalize what we think we owe in order to soften the reality of adding it all together. Each debt alone might be small, but together your debt might be larger than you'd care to know about.

So hang in there for this next worksheet. You can do this! In fact, taking a few minutes to do this next step will be very powerful in your financial turnaround.

Once you have the information gathered, and then combine it with the technique you're about to learn, you'll be amazed at the fun you'll have watching your debt go away. Yes, I said fun. Read on and you'll see what I mean.

Worksheet #13: Attack Debt

Directions: Grab your computer and dig up all those lost and forgotten usernames and passwords to your credit accounts. Gather all the necessary information about all of your debts. List the name of the debt, the total current balance that you owe, what the minimum payment is, and what you actually pay. List your debts in order from smallest to largest balance.

Debt name	Balance	Min payment	Actual payment
EXAMPLE: Car	$6,046	$333	$400
Total			

Worksheet #13 Debrief

The starting point for eliminating debt is to stop adding to it. You need a properly funded emergency fund to create a buffer between you and those unexpected events. Without enough cash in the bank you might be tempted to use credit.

Steps to eliminate debt:

1. Establish a properly funded emergency fund.
2. Stop adding to your debt.
3. Gather all the information about your debt. Use Worksheet #13.
4. Pay the minimum on all debts except the smallest.
5. Throw all the cash you can at the smallest debt.
6. When that debt is paid off, move on to the next largest debt.
7. Throw all the money you were using to pay the previous debt(s) at the new smallest debt, *plus* the minimum payment you usually make.
8. Repeat steps 4-7 until you are debt free.

Read more here: http://en.wikipedia.org/wiki/Debt-snowball_method.

A sense of accomplishment will fill you with motivation when you see your total debt drop like a rock. You will be using this new process each month and it will be a thrill to watch the totals approach zero. Stay encouraged. You can do this!

As the smaller debts go away, you will be putting more and more toward the bigger debts that you still owe. As you are able to pay more and more, the balances go to zero faster and faster. Hence the term "Debt Snowball." Now that *is* fun!

If you need more help with your debt, visit BeatnikBudget.com/Bonus for more debt resources.

The debtor is slave to the lender.
Proverbs 22:7

Get to the root cause

If you have debt, what are two specific reasons why you do?

_____

_____

_____

Are you sinking further into debt or are you making progress?

_____

_____

_____

What are the consequences of remaining in debt?

_____

_____

_____

What are the results of becoming debt free?

_____

_____

_____

What has your debt prevented you from doing in the past, and what is it preventing you from doing now?

_____

_____

_____

It may take a long time to pay off your debt. How can you stay motivated to make continual progress?

_____

_____

_____

Celebrate your milestones

Becoming debt free is more possible than you realized. You can definitely do this.

What will it feel like to send in that last payment?

_____

_____

_____

Who can you count on to help keep you accountable?

_____

_____

_____

Write yourself a quick note outlining what you believe about your ability to pay off all of your debt.

_____

_____

_____

Without enough cash in the bank you might be tempted to use credit. Build a proper emergency fund so that you have options other than debt.

Yes! We're getting there. Let's explore the difference between wants and needs. Another powerful concept that will help you reach your goals.

Step 14: Survive, Maintain, Thrive

> ## Worksheet Goal: Draw lines between different types of expenses. Use these lines to guide your spending decisions.

Now that you are getting a good grasp on your monthly expenses, you can start refining your spending plan. Take good care of the new plants that are coming up from those new roots you have planted. No more weeds, only beautiful flowers from now on.

We can get caught up in the routines of daily life and easily forget that we actually choose to take each action that we do. Yep, you chose to get out of bed today, to put on those clothes, and to read this book. You are the one who will make each and every decision for your life from now on. Get better at making choices and you will more often reap the results that you want. Once we realize we have the power to make those choices, it gets easier to decide how to spend money. Be proactive.

This worksheet will help you set some priorities around how you spend your money. You'll soon find that once you have your priorities in mind, gaining control of your spending becomes much easier.

Directions: Write down each major expense that you have identified so far. Refer to Worksheet #10 for a list of expenses to divvy up between the three columns. Add anything you feel needs to be included. Use your own judgment on this worksheet. You decide which category is most fitting for each expense. Use the guidelines below.

- Survive: Things you need to literally survive e.g. food, clothing, shelter.
- Maintain: Things you need to make your daily life function e.g. car, utilities, and insurance.
- Thrive: All the fun stuff that makes life worth living e.g. restaurants, vacations, and entertainment.

Worksheet #14: Survive, Maintain, Thrive

Survive	Maintain	Thrive
Housing	*Car*	*Movies*

Worksheet #14 Debrief

You get to choose. You are in charge. Feels good, doesn't it?

As we go about our days, weeks, months, and years, we rarely need to draw a distinction between our wants and needs. It's rarely necessary or required of us. All of our spending is thrown into one pile labeled, "Things I Bought," or "Stuff." Throwing everything into the same pile doesn't help you make distinctions. Thinking about a nice dinner as being the same as paying your car insurance doesn't help you make smart decisions. Treating them the same is like placing the same value and priority on two very different expenses. Each dollar looks the same, but the choices you make with that money should be considered for what they really are. Money is only a marker for the real things in your life.

Creating your own hierarchy of needs helps to define the lines drawn between the different categories – Survive vs. Maintain vs. Thrive. These lines are there all the time; we just don't see them, think about them, or consider them when making financial decisions. Once we see the categories clearly defined on paper, we can decide just how necessary each expense really is and then place an appropriate value on it.

You might have to temporarily (or permanently) cut down on extras in order to reach other goals. Don't think of it as a step backwards. It's quite the opposite. It's actually a step forward to know you have the basics covered and under control so you can accomplish greater goals.

You can live a balanced life full of wonderful extras and take care of all your needs at the same time. It is very straightforward. Simply take charge, make adjustments, and create a plan that works for you. You will enjoy the extras more, once you know that everything else is properly taken care of and everything is in balance.

 ## Get to the root cause

- -

How can separating your expenses into categories by priority help you make spending decisions?

_____

_____

_____

Why is it important to prioritize your spending?

_____

_____

Celebrate your milestones

You can gain greater control over your spending when you are mindful of your priorities. Balance in any area of life is important, including finances.

What thoughts came to mind after taking a look at how you are prioritizing your spending?

_____

_____

_____

Will being conscious of items you need vs. items you don't need contribute to the success of your financial turnaround? How do you see this awareness benefiting you long term?

_____

_____

_____

Is the survive, maintain, thrive concept applicable to any other area of life? How can it change the way you think about the way you spend your time?

_____

_____

_____

How does it feel to have one more step completed? Write down a few adjectives that summarize how it feels to know you've made the decision to be intentional with your money.

_____

_____

Wonderful! Just one more for the week. This next one is super powerful and creates less work for you from now on.

Step 15: Make It Automatic

> **Worksheet Goal:** Make life easier by setting your finances to run automatically.

Make your financial machine work automatically so you can enjoy a little stress relief. Automating financial tasks reduces the amount of time and energy spent on the whole operation.

Most employers offer automatic direct deposit for your paycheck. What about your bills, giving, savings, investing, and debt payments? They can also be set up to happen automatically.

There are many reasons to automate these tasks. Here are a few:

- Save time
- Reduce stress from thinking and worrying
- Eliminate the possibility of missing a payment
- No more guessing if you are saving enough
- No more guessing if you are investing enough for retirement
- Put another barrier between you and your money
- Makes reaching your goals effortless and automatic, a guarantee

David Bach wrote an entire book about this idea. It's called *The Automatic Millionaire* and it is a wonderful book. It is incredibly simple and powerful. I tell people about this book all the time. I am telling you about it right now, go read it!

finishrich.com/books/automatic_brandhome.php

Worksheet #15: Make It Automatic

Directions: Make a list of tasks that you can automate, the steps you need to take to arrange the service, and the date you completed the task.

Task to automate	How to do it	Date completed
Example: $100 a month into mutual fund	*Set up auto-withdraw account*	*9-22-2013*

Worksheet # 15 Debrief

Many people contribute to a retirement account at work. The money is automatically taken out of your paycheck before you can get your hands on it. Because of this, you can't spend that retirement allotment. It doesn't feel like it's even there. It doesn't even feel like it belongs to you. There is a barrier between this kind of money and you.

Notice how it only *feels* unavailable. This feeling has been created because of the automatic deduction process. You experience it as though it's in some bank account, far, far away on another planet. Create a physical barrier between you and your money and you often create a stronger emotional barrier at the same time. The result is a system that works for you and helps you reach your goals faster.

Lots of people wouldn't dare touch the money in a 401(k). If that is you, why not put a little more in there? Or, set up another investment account with an automatic withdraw function. You won't touch that extra money either and you'll thank yourself later.

Do the same with your debt payments. Set up a system that automatically pays your debt payment each month. And remember to adjust the amounts based on your debt snowball strategy.

Get to the root cause

- -

Name two specific reasons to set payments up to be drafted automatically.

_____

_____

What specific goals could you reach sooner and more easily simply by setting up automatic deposit or withdrawal authorizations?

_____

_____

_____

Celebrate your milestones

It's a big relief to know that the bills are paid on time. It's a wonderful feeling to know that your retirement account is being funded automatically, behind the scenes, without your involvement. You have a plan to make it all happen even easier – and with less stress – by setting up a system to take care of it all automatically.

What will you do with all the extra time now that you won't need to spend it writing checks, licking envelopes, and double checking to make sure all bills are paid?

_____

_____

_____

What does streamlining your entire financial situation feel like?

_____

_____

Perfect! You're on the home stretch. Another week down, just one more and you're well on your way to a financial future that you will love. Your financial turnaround is almost complete.

Week Three Goals and Action Steps

Before we stop for the week, think about what ideas came to mind while you were making progress. I imagine you have had lots of great ideas, asked some great questions, and thought of some great answers. Translate those ideas into *one specific goal* you would like to accomplish. Then write down *one specific action step* that you can take *this week* to get closer to achieving that goal.

Worksheet 11 – Sell it for cash

Goal _____

Action step _____

Worksheet 12 – Extra income

Goal _____

Action step _____

Worksheet 13 - Debt

Goal _____

Action step _____

Worksheet 14 – Survival

Goal _____

Action step _____

Worksheet 15 – Automatic

Goal _____

Action step _____

Week Three Summary and Conclusion

Things are looking up. Reconstruction gives you a stronger foundation to operate on.

- You got a jumpstart on your emergency fund, savings, or debt by selling some stuff for cash. Doing this created energy that fueled motivation. That motivation is transferable to other areas of this process. Use that cash wisely, and use that motivation to propel you forward.

- One of the ways to make faster progress is to make some extra cash. Dieting alone works slowly. Dieting plus exercise rocks! You came up with some ways to make this happen. Temporary work that leads to permanent success.

- Organizing your debt is a powerful process. With all the information centralized and organized, you created a plan of attack. Becoming debt free is close at hand.

- This week you also defined the difference between things you need to survive, maintain, and thrive while you are here on this planet. Drawing lines between these categories will help you make better choices and bring clarity to your decision making.

- By setting certain financial tasks to occur automatically, you helped simplify your life by decreasing "mental clutter." You also created helpful automatic structures between you and the money you would like to save. These structures will help you achieve your goals faster and with minimal continuous effort on your part.

The only way to get better at golf or the piano is to practice, practice, practice. The same is true for money and budgeting. Learn about your current situation. Identify the weak spots. Discover what needs to change. Practice changing these habits and new, healthier habits will form.

Week three is over!

Congratulations! You are in rare company.
Welcome to the elite group of financially mindful and successful people.
You might still have a long road ahead of you, but you ARE successful NOW.
If you have made it this far I want to say congratulations personally.

Go to this web address for a fun video just for you.
BeatnikBudget.com/FourWeekSpecialVideo.

Week 1   Week 2   Week 3   Week 4

Week Four

WEEK FOUR: ONE WORKSHEET TO RULE THEM ALL

Creating an Airtight Monthly Budget

Introduction and goal: This is the week we've been building up to. The moment we have all been waiting for. It's time to create a simple and powerful monthly budget that won't just work. It will rock!

Welcome to the beginning of a powerful new habit, a healthy habit that will produce healthy results. Just like exercising every day makes you physically healthy, working your budget each month produces healthy financial results.

Before each month starts you can now use these new tools to plan how you will spend your money. It's important to get into the habit of writing it down on paper. This helps you stay on track. Make the shift from being reactive to being proactive with your money.

When each month comes to an end, you will also want to revisit your bank statement and compare how close your actual spending was to what you budgeted. You will be able to calculate the difference between what you budgeted and what you actually spent. Once you get this number you can make the needed adjustments to improve the next month. Continual improvement will get you closer to your goals faster and more consistently. It's like having a GPS system for your money – the system will now help you stay on course.

Step 16: The Monthly Budget

> ## Worksheet Goal: Create a plan for your money that gives you peace of mind, gained from knowing your plan will work.

Directions: Start with your income and split it up between the following categories. Keep your goals in mind while you do this. Strike a balance between your goals and what you are able to realistically achieve.

Use the columns on Worksheet #16 as described.

Budgeted: This is the plan that you (and your spouse/partner/accountability buddy/etc.) have defined. Total your income, and then allocate that amount between the categories listed below. Work with your partner on your plan.

Actual: At the end of the month, print off your bank statement and account for every purchase line by line, putting every purchase into a category and recording the totals.

Difference: For the spending categories, you will subtract the actual amounts from the budgeted amounts. On the income line, you will subtract the budgeted from the actuals. When you see how far above or below your target you are, you can make educated adjustments in your purchasing behavior each month. As the months go by, the numbers from the ACTUAL column will get closer and closer to the numbers in the BUDGETED column. (Practice, Practice, Practice.)

Total each page as you go. Add up the three spending totals to get a spending grand total. Subtract the spending grand total from your income. What do you see? It should equal zero. If it is more than zero, you forgot to allocate some of your income. In this case, it is a good idea to put the un-allocated amount into the Savings or Unexpected column. If it is less than zero, you have planned to spend more money than you will earn this month. If so, are you able to handle it without credit cards and debt?

Worksheet #16: The Monthly Budget

MONTH:	$ Budgeted	$ Actual	$ Difference
Income			
SPENDING:	$ Budgeted	$ Actual	$ Difference
Giving			
Cash withdrawal			
Rent / mortgage			
Bill #1			
Bill #2			
Bill #3			
Bill #4			
Bill #5			
Bill #6			
Phone			
Page 1 spending total			

	$ Budgeted	$ Actual	$ Difference
Grocery			
Restaurant			
*Emergency fund			
*4 Months' expenses			
*Car replacement			
*Insurance			
*Medical			
*Holidays			
*Clothing			
*Vacation			
*Household items			
Debt #1			
Debt #2			
Debt #3			
Student loan			
Car: gas / oil / repair			
Page 2 total			

	$ Budgeted	$ Actual	$ Difference
Entertainment			
Gifts			
Investing / retirement			
Hobby			
Alcohol / cigs / vices			
Other			
Other			
Unexpected #1			
Unexpected #2			
Unexpected #3			
Page 3 total			
Pages 1+2+3 total			
Subtract total spending from total income			
Equals (Should equal zero)	$0	$0	$0

These represent your savings categories.
Again, make sure you subtracted the budgeted from the actual on the income line only.

The Monthly Budget Recap

Keep it up: Do a budget every month for a year. Notice how much things improve over time. It takes 30 days to form a habit. It takes a bit longer in this case, but healthy spending habits can be created. If you stick with it, the development of healthy habits is a guarantee. It gets easier and goes quicker the more you practice. Remember, the goal isn't to make the math add up perfectly. The goal is to form healthy spending habits.

Be conservative: When you fill out the Budgeted column each month, plan for things to be ten percent more expensive than you think they will be. This way, when things go well you will be pleasantly surprised. When things do go wrong, it won't be too difficult to deal with; you will have it covered. You have to stay ahead of your money or you will always feel behind.

Savings: You may have noticed there is no savings category. I tricked you. There are actually nine savings categories. Check out the bonus worksheet entitled, Savings Goals for Your Monthly Budget, for the explanation.

Your free gift: Download the interactive PDF of this workbook if you haven't yet. Go to BeatnikBudget.com/FreeFourWeekpdf, to get it. You can easily add new categories or change the names of the categories to fit your situation. It will even do the math for you. Now that you have paid your dues using pen and paper, let the computer help out. Use the PDF over and over each month.

I'd like to wrap this week up by offering you more encouragement, helping you set some goals and offering you a wealth of budgeting tips.

Get to the root cause

Every dollar that you spend, save, give, or invest touches your hands first. A decision was made concerning each dollar. A monthly budget is the best tool available to help you make an educated decision on how to go about spending, saving, giving, and investing. It's your money, you worked hard to earn it, and you should be the one making the decisions.

If you really want to make a serious commitment to a better financial future, write down *ten reasons why* doing a monthly budget is a *smart idea*. Then write down *ten goals* that doing a monthly budget will help you reach. Then *ten action steps* that will help you get closer to your goals. Find these worksheets on the next three pages. Feel free to repeat some of the goals and actions from the previous weeks.

Celebrate your milestones

This is a major milestone. It's definitely time to celebrate. Take a minute to give yourself a round of applause and perhaps a high five. You deserve it. In fact, I have something special for you here: BeatnikBudget.com/StandingOvation.

What does taking control and being proactive with your money mean to you? What does it say about your commitment to having a future that you can be proud of?

_____

_____

_____

What will taking control and being proactive allow you to accomplish?

_____

_____

_____

Tell someone! You deserve to celebrate after all of your hard work!

10 Reasons Why Doing a Monthly Budget is a Smart Idea

1.
2.
3.
4.
5.
6.
7.
8.
9.
10.

10 Goals That a Budget Will Help You Achieve

1.

2.

3.

4.

5.

6.

7.

8.

9.

10.

*Anything worth doing is worth doing poorly
until you can learn to do it well.*
-Zig Ziglar

10 Action Steps That Will Help You Reach Your Goals

1.
2.
3.
4.
5.
6.
7.
8.
9.
10.

In all things success depends on previous preparation.
-Confucius

Common Pitfalls, Black Holes, Things to Avoid

Food: The biggest black hole. Eating out for breakfast, lunch, and dinner is an enormous money grabber. Drinking coffee, soda, alcohol, bottled water, and energy drinks is also an enormous money pit. Snacks and drinks from the vending machine, gas station, or drive through also add up fast. BONUS: Most of these things are unhealthy and unnecessary anyway. Making just a few specific changes here will add up to major savings. You might even realize that life is better without them.

Entertainment: Movies, shows, sporting events, gambling, concerts. Fun can be free. It's whom you are with, not where you are and what you are doing that makes it fun. You might even agree that some of your best memories did not come with a price tag. Some of the biggest disappointments come with an equally big price tag. When family and friends visit from out of town, you don't have to spend a mountain of money to entertain them. You don't have to spend money at all to be entertained and have fun. The entertainment industry spends a lot of time trying to convince you otherwise, but you see right through it, don't you?

Subscriptions: How many monthly bills are automatic subscription-style services? How many of those can you cancel, right now? Examine each one and ask yourself if you are getting your money's worth. Ask yourself if you really need it. Can you do without it for a year? You might even realize that life is better without these things and that you didn't really even want them. Cable TV is a choice, not a requirement. Can you cancel your cable bill for a year or two, get your money right, and then think about hooking your cable back up? You don't have to go without forever.

Impulse buys: How many things do you buy every week that you didn't plan for in advance? If less than one hour passes between your first thought of making a purchase and actually making that purchase, it is an impulse buy. Ask yourself if the purchase you are about to make is covered in your monthly budget. If so, go for it and enjoy it. If not, don't do it. Keep track of these impulse buys. Focus on the most expensive five items throughout the month. Small changes here will add up to big results. Each decision that you make should be predetermined and based on moving closer to your goals. Good planning will make each decision easier to make.

Debt and payments: Debt is your enemy. Get rid of all your debt. Payments are like shackles. Get rid of all your payments. Pay cash for cars. Break the shackles. Don't make payments on TVs, furniture, or appliances. Crush your debt; it is holding you back. Debt is not a helping hand. Debt is a product that someone invented to make a profit off people who try to buy things that they can't afford. Debt is a trap. Debt is wrong. Debt is a trick. Debt is unnecessary. Debt has clear winners and clear losers.

Holidays, vacation, and travel: The holidays come every year at the same time, no surprises there. Create a line on your budget for the holidays and use it. If you spend $1,200 during the holidays (gifts, travel, meals, entertainment included) you should set aside $100 a month to save up for it. Don't let it sneak up on you. Avoid using credit and paying for these expenses the rest of the year. Births, birthdays, vacations, reunions, weddings, showers, funerals - there are plenty of reasons to travel. Have a plan for these events, too. It shouldn't be a "surprise." Plan for these events ahead of time, they will pop up over and over throughout your entire lifetime. These recurring events require smart, continuous, ongoing planning in advance. Having these events covered financially will add to your already growing peace of mind.

Gifts and giving: How many weddings, wedding showers, baby showers, birthdays, funerals (with flowers and travel), care calendars, housewarming parties, disaster relief efforts, and other gift-giving opportunities will present themselves this year? How about the next 20 years? At $50 a pop, plus travel, giving gets expensive, fast. Are you putting enough on the gifts line on your budget? Set enough money aside each month to cover these expenses. When these events do occur, you won't have to wonder where the money will come from. The money will be sitting there waiting for you.

"Unexpected": There are countless surprise expenses waiting around every corner. "But that never happens," or, "I didn't see that coming" are not very good plans. You will find that no one is listening anyway. (Those are reactive plans that don't work, you are a proactive person and therefore need a better plan.) There are so many things that only happen once in a lifetime, so many that two or three of them will happen every month. You must be proactive when it comes to planning for unexpected expenses. Because you can't see them coming doesn't mean you can't plan for them. Expect the unexpected and when the unexpected happens, you will have it covered. Put a dollar amount on the unexpected line on your budget every month. Something will happen, are you prepared? You will need to do this every month. This is the best way to guarantee that you won't spend that money on something else before the unexpected event happens. Remember, it's not that you 'don't have the money,' you did have the money but spent it on something else.

You should have three layers of cushion for unexpected events:

1. Emergency fund
2. 3-6 months of expenses
3. Monthly unexpected

THINGS TO REMEMBER

The goal: The goal *is not* to create the perfect budget and get the numbers exact every time. The goal is to *create healthy spending habits.* Every now and then, the numbers just won't add up. Don't let that distract you from the real goal, creating healthy spending habits. The numbers are important, but realize that there is a difference between the process and the goal. While you could choose to manage your money using tally marks on your living room wall, the goal should be the same: creating healthy spending habits. Use the method that works best for you. Always remember the big picture, your vision and your goals. Don't get too caught up in the math, numbers, details, and spreadsheets. Those are all tools, not goals.

Keep it simple: Keeping it simple will allow you to maintain a better grasp of what is going on – you'll be able to see from start to finish exactly what your money is doing. As a result, you will be better able to make a positive impact on the situation. If your budgeting method gets too complicated, you run the risk of getting overwhelmed and abandoning the entire thing. You won't be able to see where you need to make changes and how to go about creating those changes. It is crucial to have a complete mental image of how the different parts fit together. A short and simple budget that you understand and use is infinitely more powerful than a complicated budget that you don't understand or use. This budgeting process will work 99% of the time for 99% of the people who use it. We tend to make it more complex and difficult than it has to be. You aren't intimidated, not you. You are in control. Keeping it simple will allow you to focus on the important parts of the process. That focus will allow you to make continuous progress towards your goals.

Repetition: Creating and sticking to a budget every month is one of the best things you can do for yourself, your family, and your dependents. We owe it to ourselves, our families, and to society at large to be good stewards of the money we have been blessed with the job of managing. Getting yourself into a mess affects more than just you. It also affects those around you. You may have learned a lot of new information here, especially those of you who have *never* worked a budget. It might not have gone very well. Maybe it was a big mess and didn't look very pretty. Don't worry. You cannot do a budget one time and expect things to change forever. Just like diet and exercise, the progress adds up over time. And if you stop exercising, you will feel the negative effects within a few weeks. It is also much easier to stay in shape than it is to get in shape. Hang in there and repeat, repeat, repeat. Within a quick three or four months, a few important things will happen.

- *You will memorize all of your bills, debts, payments, spending, giving, saving, and investing information.* Your ship could have holes in it, be taking on water and about to sink and you might not realize it until it is too late to do anything about it. Imagine having complete knowledge of every square inch of that ship. Memorize all the current and potential leaks and when the ship begins to take on water you will know exactly where to look for the leaks and exactly how to make the repairs.

- *It gets easier* - much, much easier. Hang in there. The first month can be hard. Like learning any new skill, it can be challenging and confusing at first, but after a few months you will be become much more comfortable with the process.

- *It gets faster* - much, much faster. After a few months it should take about one hour (or less) a month to keep up with your monthly budget.

- *Magic:* You will notice something magical begin to happen, especially during the first few months. Subconsciously, just because you have been thinking about your money and where it is going, your spending habits will change. You'll notice that you end each month with more and more money in the bank. Awareness leads to action and action leads to results. Remember the coaching clients that I mentioned? They have noticed and told me that month four is the magic month. Month four is when the results appear out of nowhere with tremendous power!

Sleep: It is a great feeling to rest easy at night. A few years back a friend of mine, Chris, realized that his debt was getting unmanageable. Chris would lay in bed awake at night thinking about his growing debt. He literally thought that there was no way out and that he would be in debt his entire life. He would just lie there, totally consumed with the feeling of being trapped with no way out. He realized that he needed to take care of this growing problem. He started making some changes and realized that he could turn things around. Chris saw the benefits of taking charge and making smarter decisions. He created a plan of action and paid off all of his debt. It's much easier for Chris to sleep now that he has won this battle. Chris took control and won the war, battle by battle. So can you.

It is never too late: Starting now will produce positive results faster than you might think. It's never too late to take charge and gain better control over your finances. Start now. Start today. If your past is full of poor financial decisions, don't let that prevent you from moving forward. It's never too late to break free of the past and start creating a new and better future. Hit the reset button. Then hit the restart button.

It is never too early: Take charge early and often. If the best time to start was yesterday, the second best time to start is right now. Right now is always a good time to start. Your future is written with the decisions you make between now and then. Think "future-success" with every decision you make and your future will be a great place to arrive.

It is never hopeless: No matter how desperate a situation appears to be, it can almost always be turned around (in just four weeks!). Try a few of these options in the place of worry, fear, anxiety, and defeat.

- *Keep a positive mental attitude always:* No matter how bad the situation might get. Don't let anyone else or any situation determine your state of mind.
- *Get support:* Gather a team of supporters such as an accountability partner or even a network of people who are on your team. Have monthly or quarterly meet-ups to keep each other on track and motivated. My newsletter, "The Newsletter That Loves You," is a great accountability partner. Sign up on my website, BeatnikBudget.com.
- *Always keep the future in mind:* If things are tough now, don't let your current set of circumstances hold you back from a future that is full of success. What you believe about the future affects the way you think and act now. Do you believe there is a better future ahead? Are your thoughts and actions in line with creating that desired future? Do you believe that your plan will work? If so, are you acting like your plan will work? And finally, do you believe that you can reach your goals? If so, are you acting like it and making choices that will help you reach your goals?

More than monthly: Bills and expenses that occur on a monthly cycle are the easiest to plan for. They line up with the monthly budgeting cycle nicely, therefore making it easy to visualize and plan for. Expenses that occur more than once a month can add up unnoticed. Because we pay for these expenses in small bits and pieces, it can be difficult to see the impact that these more frequent expenses have. A monthly coffee or grocery store bill would provide a better image of the reality of the situation. Adding them up to get monthly grand totals is the best way to see them for what they truly are. Although small, they add up to very large expenses. Keep a close eye on these smaller expenses. We always spend our money one dollar at a time. But sometimes those dollars are in groups of 20 or 200 or more. A dollar is a dollar, no matter how many are in the group, 1 or 100. Think of each one dollar purchase as a one hundred dollar purchase that is spread out over a period of time. How will that affect your choices?

Less than monthly: Bills and expenses that occur less than once a month can sneak up on you and find you unprepared. Bills like medical expenses, holidays, insurance, taxes, and a new car, to name just a few. These expenses are also hard to visualize for what they truly are. They must be planned for monthly, throughout the year. You must create a monthly plan that blends together the monthly, less than monthly, and more than monthly expenses. The next bonus worksheet will help with those less than monthly expenses.

The results (the true goal): The true goal is *peace of mind.* Being able to rest easy when it comes to your money. Life is far too short and way too long to carry money problems around with you the whole time. Too many relationships are harmed as a result of making poor money choices. Remember to dig deeper and go beyond the choices. Find the root cause. Explore your reactions too. You can't control the unexpected events but you can prepare for them. You can also choose your reactions. Your preparation and your choices have the greatest impact on your results, greater than the events of your life. Unhealthy and unwanted financial choices and outcomes are usually the end result of a long series of previous events, choices, and reactions. Make wise choices. Deal with the root causes and you won't have to spend so much time repairing the unnecessary damage. You can rest easy and focus on other areas of your life knowing that your plan and proactive approach to money has planted the seeds for your own peace of mind.

Congratulations! You completed your four-week financial turnaround!

Make a new budget every month for the next 100 years.
Enjoy the ongoing feeling of success as you continue to make progress.
Have fun with it.

Week 1   Week 2   Week 3   Week 4

BONUS! Savings Goals for Your Monthly Budget

It's not enough to just have a savings. Remember the concept from Worksheet #5? You've got to give a name to each and every dollar you have in savings. Together, these nine categories represent your savings. Feel free to add more if you need to.

Directions:

- List the item, the item's cost, and how many months away the purchase date is.
- Divide the purchase price by the number of months until you plan to purchase the item.
- Make each item a category on your monthly budget.
- Save the amount listed each month until the goal is met or the item is purchased.

Example:

Item	Total cost	Months until purchase/funded	Monthly amount to save
Emergency fund	$2,000	12	$167
4 months' expenses	$5,000	36	$139
New car	$5,000	72	$70
Yearly insurance	$500	12	$42
Medical	$1,000	12	$83
Holidays	$1,000	12	$83
Clothing	$500	8	$63
Vacation	$2,000	16	$125
Housing	$1,000	16	$63
Other			
Other			
Other			
Total	$18,000		$835

Savings Goals Exercise

Item	Total cost	Months until purchase	Monthly amount to save
Emergency fund			
4 months' expenses			
New car			
Yearly insurance			
Medical			
Holidays			
Clothing			
Vacation			
Housing			
Other			
Other			
Other			
Total			

Download your own electronic version of this worksheet here:
BeatnikBudget.com/Bonus.

SUMMARY AND NEXT STEPS

A monthly budget is the most powerful tool in your financial toolbox; it will help you get the most out of the money you earn. There are no short cuts. Success must be earned through discipline, habits, repetition, dedication, and hard work. It takes time.

Budgeting comes first and investing comes second. You can't put $200 a month in a mutual fund or retirement account if you don't have $200 because you spent it. You have to control your money first (budget) before you can teach it to do tricks (investments). Every dollar you earn and spend should flow through your budget. Your budget is like central command for every other department in your financial business. All the orders for every dollar come from central command. Everything your money will ever do, complex and simple, should be decided ahead of time and properly accounted for on your monthly budget.

You can't become debt free if you spend your money on other things. Control your money first (budget) and then teach it to pay off your debt quickly.

Control your money while it is in your hands. Create barriers between you and the money that you want to save. Don't let the money that you worked so hard to earn slip through your fingers. Realize that you have created your current situation and you have the power to make the changes you see fit.

Now that you have completed this entire workbook, uncovering the facts and details of your situation, go ahead and write down a few more goals and action steps. Draw from the previous goals and action steps. Add more goals and action steps that are oriented toward your future success. What do you want to accomplish this month, this quarter, or this year? How about creating a five year plan? What are your lifetime and retirement goals?

If you don't dream it first, it won't happen. But if you *can and do* dream it, the sky is the limit and you can achieve whatever your mind can dream up.

Yearly Goals

What would you like to achieve in the next 12 months?

1.	
2.	
3.	
4.	
5.	
6.	
7.	
8.	
9.	
10.	

The important thing about having goals is having them.

-Geoffrey F. Albert

Five Year Plan

What do you want your situation to look like in five years?

1.	
2.	
3.	
4.	
5.	
6.	
7.	
8.	
9.	
10.	

Lifetime and Retirement Goals

What are your long-term goals?

1.
2.
3.
4.
5.
6.
7.
8.
9.
10.

Extra Bonus!

Let me tell you a little secret. There is a hidden page on my website that has a bunch of useful resources and products. I update this page every now and then so you will want to check back once a month to see what is new. There are three very important things you should know about this page.

1. In my newsletter I always include an update about new resources on this secret page. Sign up for the newsletter at BeatnikBudget.com.

2. I pay very close attention to my readers. I love you guys!! Most of my products and resources are in direct response to questions and requests from people just like you. Please feel free to email me and tell me exactly how I can help you. If I haven't already addressed the issue, you can be sure a blog post or a new product or resource will come of it shortly. Contact me anytime with your ideas.
   Derek@BeatnikBudget.com.

3. Here is the link to that amazing bonus page I keep yapping about:
   BeatnikBudget.com/Bonus.

There you have it, a page of free bonus material that is always being updated!

Shhhh, lets keep this page between you and I.

SPEAKING OF...

Speaking:

I am available to speak at your event. Seminars, conferences, churches, schools, groups, and events of most kinds. Are you looking for a dynamic speaker that will help make your conference successful and memorable? If the message of your event and my unique style are a match, I'd love to hear from you. Let's discuss your goals and how I can contribute to the vision of your event. BeatnikBudget.com/Speaking.

Workshops:

Live workshops can add great value. I can provide on-site, single and multi-session workshops for your business, association, or event. BeatnikBudget.com/Workshops.

Coaching: (For Individuals and Groups)

Need an experienced helping hand? I would love to be on your team. I have been there, done that, and made it through. Together, we will create a plan that works for you. From anywhere in the world, we can meet up and get things done using phone, video, email, or in person (Kansas City only). One-on-one coaching is the highest level of attention you can get. Coaching works. Get from where you are now to where you want to be faster than you would on your own. BeatnikBudget.com/Coaching.

Interviews:

As you can probably tell, I have a lot to say about money management. My wife and I have an exciting story with a happy ending. We have used our story to inspire and encourage many people. If my message is one that your audience will benefit from, please contact me.

BeantikBudget.com/Story.

Media Kit:

Please visit BeatnikBudget.com/Media to view our media kit.

Blog Posts and Articles:

Looking for a guest blog post or an article for your publication? I do a select few each month. Contact me anytime and let's see what we can accomplish together.

Bulk Orders:

Bulk orders of *The Four Week Financial Turnaround* are available. Contact me for special bulk order pricing. Schools, financial coaches, financial study groups, pre-marital counseling, educators, pastors, and students of all kinds. If you need a stack of books, I would love to make that happen.

Amazon:

Have you enjoyed this book? Tell us and the rest of the world about it. Likes, stars, and honest reviews on Amazon are encouraged and much appreciated. Thanks! Help spread the word by leaving your thoughts about this book. Go to Amazon.com and search for *The Four Week Financial Turnaround*, or type this address into your favorite browser:

http://www.amazon.com/The-Four-Week-Financial-Turnaround/dp/0985886307

ABOUT THE AUTHOR

Derek C. Olsen believes in big ideas that can change your life for the better in substantial ways.

Derek transitioned to the life of an entrepreneur in January of 2011 with the creation of Beatnik Budget. As founder of Beatnik Budget, he made it his mission to help others achieve their financial goals. Derek is the author of *The Four Week Financial Turnaround*, a speaker on the subject of money management and marriage, and facilitator of both financial and career-related workshops. His hobbies include reading, cycling, music, brainstorming and enjoying desserts of all kinds.

Derek grew up in the Oklahoma City area. He earned a B.S. degree in business management from Oklahoma State University. After graduation, Derek spent six years as a territorial sales manager in both the Oklahoma City and Kansas City markets. Derek's love for helping others with personal finance and money management pours out through his ideas, products, speaking and life. Happily married to Carrie since October of 2010, Derek calls Kansas City home.

Derek's belief in the people he inspires can be wrapped up in one of his favorite encouraging sentences, *"You can do it, and I would love to help."*

Reach Derek at Derek@beatnikbudget.com

HIS+*Hers*
=OUR$

Fight together. Not each other.

Carrie and I got married weeks before we almost lost our house in a foreclosure. The feeling of helplessness we experienced was paralyzing. We made it through a long, fearful season. Along the way, we learned that when the ground gets shaky, you have to fight together, not each other.

Money can be a uniting force in your relationship. Don't wait another moment: work together to build a worry-free, secure and rewarding future.

-Derek C. Olsen

Book. Workbook. Community.
HisPlusHersEqualsOurs.com

Made in the USA
San Bernardino, CA
01 June 2013